Praise Fo

Your Business, Your Family, Your Legacy

"Managing a family business goes so far beyond maintaining peace over the Thanksgiving turkey. Drawing on his long experience, George Isaac provides essential wisdom for establishing a legacy that will survive from generation to generation."

HARVEY MACKAY

#1 *New York Times* bestselling author of *Swim with the Sharks Without Being Eaten Alive*

"George Isaac's book provides a unique and valuable contribution to family enterprises. He combines his expertise as a consultant for Deloitte with his practical experience of managing succession in his own family business as the third-generation CEO. He offers a clear perspective on the varied issues facing all multigenerational family enterprises. George highlights the challenges and gives very pragmatic and useful strategies for dealing with both the business and financial issues and the associated complex family dynamics of a family enterprise. Additionally, he incorporates succession strategies for board and management transitions, as well as valuable ideas for empowering the next generation for future leadership. If you want your enterprise to thrive, George Isaac has the road map!"

LEE HAUSNER, PHD

Internationally Recognized Family Business Consultant, Speaker, and Clinical Psychologist, Author of *Hats Off to You…Finding Success in Family Business Succession*

"Whether you are an experienced family business executive or board member, family office executive or next-generation family member interested in learning more, George Isaac has written a must-read primer on the challenges of managing a multigenerational family enterprise (defined as a family business or family office). George draws from his decades of experience as a partner at Deloitte Consulting, as CEO of The Isaac Group (his own family business), and as advisor to many multigenerational families to create a compelling how-to guide filled with best practices, checklists, and action steps to follow. Highly recommended reading!"

JAMES K. CORNELL

Managing Partner of Fiduciary Wealth Partners, Seventh-Generation Family Business Owner, Chair of the Young Presidents' Organization (YPO) Family Office Principals Group

"George Isaac has captured the essence of the family enterprise—built by family for family—and how to perpetuate it throughout generations. A great primer for this most significant sector of business—from understanding difficult financial statements to the issues of conflict, governance, and succession. It is an insider's view of how to make family business work and keep working. A must read for anyone in their family's enterprise."

JAMES G. ELLIS

Dean of the Marshall School of Business at the University of Southern California, Robert R. Dockson Dean's Chair in Business Administration

"You hold in your hands an extremely valuable tool for you, your family, and your business. George Isaac has distilled down decades of real-world knowledge—as both a high-level professional consultant and as the CEO of his family's large multigenerational business—into a readable and easy-to-follow format which provides critical information for your road map to business success. George is a born educator who has high-level consultancy experience coupled with actually running a business, which allows him to conceptualize nonconventional solutions—he is a true thought leader."

TIMOTHY LAPPEN

Founder and Chairman, The Family Office Group Jeffer Mangels Butler & Mitchell LLP, 2018 "Lawyer of the Year" for Closely Held Companies and Family-Businesses Law, LA, 2019 "Lawyer of the Year" for Trusts and Estates Law, LA

"George has put together a wonderfully concise and practical field guide for those in pursuit of a sustainable, multigenerational family enterprise. While a lot of other entries in the space are high minded, George cuts to the chase on the issues without being redundant or moralizing. The chapters on financial statements, creating business value, and avoiding the 'wealth evaporation trap' are clear, simple, and eminently useful for preparing people and systems for 'evergreen' ownership. This little book ought to be in the briefcase or (these days) smartphone of any 'family champion' who is exploring or pursuing multigenerational family ownership!"

STEVE LYTLE

Fourth-Generation Chair of The Agnew Family Ownership
Council, Past Chair of the YPO Global Family Business Network

"George Isaac was always my go-to author for articles on governing the family company, so I am delighted he has written a book that captures and conveys in clear advice and insights his impressive body of knowledge on not only family company governance but other vital aspects of managing the family enterprise—including managing family dynamics, family wealth, succession planning, and even incredibly useful tips on selling the business (if you have to). Anyone working in or associated with a family company should have this book at their fingertips for ready and frequent reference."

JAMES KRISTIE

Editor and Associate Publisher (retired) of *Directors & Boards*

"Finally! A practical family business guidebook from someone who's 'been there and done that' in managing his family's third-generation business, as well as consulting with numerous other family businesses. George knows where the family business landmines are and how to disarm them! The points covered in *Your Business, Your Family, Your Legacy* are the key points we focus on in the USC Marshall Family Business Program, where George serves as chair of our advisory board and regular lecturer. Thanks for sharing your wisdom in such a practical and understandable manner and providing a road map for family enterprise leaders and stakeholders."

KEN UDE

Director of the University of Southern California
Marshall Family Business Program

"This is an important and needed book. From interacting with many hundreds of family businesses, I believe that much of the advice in this book has three characteristics: 1) It's not widely known; 2) It's highly beneficial; and 3) It's at DEFCON 1 in importance when it comes to the survival of the family business."

MITZI PERDUE

Fourth-Generation Family Business Leader, Internationally Recognized Speaker and Advisor, and Author of *How to Make Your Family Business Last* and *Tough Man, Tender Chicken: Business and Life Lessons from Frank Perdue*

"I have had the pleasure to have known and worked professionally with George Isaac for more than twenty-five years. His deep personal experience in managing and advising substantial family businesses includes a long history in management consulting and private equity. His broad and unique perspective enables him to identify and resolve the thorny issues that face most family businesses and help leadership anticipate hidden or unspoken problems that could threaten the business's future viability. These can include family personal issues as well as business and wealth management concerns. This book is a 'must read' for all owners of a family enterprise."

ALEXANDER L. CAPPELLO

Founder, Chairman, and CEO, Cappello Global, LLC (A Leading Global Investment Bank to the Middle Market); International Board Chairman (prior), YPO; and Board Chairman/Lead Director of Numerous Publicly Traded and Privately Held Companies in the U.S. & Overseas

Your
BUSINESS

Your
FAMILY

Your
LEGACY

Building a Multigenerational Family Business That Lasts

George A. Isaac

amplify

www.amplifypublishing.com

Your Business, Your Family, Your Legacy

For more information, please contact:
Mascot Books
620 Herndon Parkway #320
Herndon, VA 20170
info@mascotbooks.com

Library of Congress Control Number: 2019903724

CPSIA Code: PRFRE0619A
ISBN-13: 978-1-64307-565-5

Printed in Canada

To Shari, my wife of thirty-seven years, for supporting and contributing to my personal life journey and business success.

To my parents, Lilly and George Isaac Jr., who taught me many important life and business lessons.

To our children, Megan, Drew, and his wife Julie, who perpetuate our family traditions and values for Gen 4.

To our young grandchild, George V, and future descendants, who will hopefully carry our family values for Gen 5 and beyond.

And to my brother Zac, always by my side as my life business partner and best friend.

CONTENTS

PREFACE

MANY OF THE GIANT public companies of today began as private family companies. Several continue to carry the names of their founding families: DowDuPont, Ford Motor, Johnson & Johnson, JPMorgan Chase, Goldman Sachs, Disney, and Hewlett-Packard, to name a few.

Unfortunately, many large US public corporations have become impersonal and have lost their historical sense of "family" and the singular high values that generally inspire and drive family companies. Subsequent downsizing, rightsizing, mergers, spinoffs, and business failures of many large public companies devastate many families through lost jobs or static incomes.

Today, privately owned small and midsized companies are even more important than ever. They represent 50 percent of the private sector of the US economy (and private workforce), according to the US Small Business Administration's "2018 Small Business Profile." Small and midsized companies, many of which are family businesses, generate *two-thirds* of all job growth and are the backbone of the US economy and working families.

Nonetheless, family businesses face great challenges to their survival and growth because they must manage the often-treacherous shoals of family relationships through succeeding generations. The difficulties are well illustrated by the startling statistic that only 10 to 15 percent of family businesses in the US make it to the third generation.

The goal of this book is to show family business owners how to avoid the pitfalls that trap and destroy both young and mature family businesses. I hope it will convince you that family businesses remain the best opportunity to create wealth and provide rewarding lives to many stakeholders.

My Personal Family Business Journey

I have lived the family business life for sixty-five years! My personal experiences growing up, literally next door to "the office," provided treasured memories and a real sense of being part of a family business enterprise.

I was born in Bryan, Ohio—a town of around 7,500 people. Our family business was started by my immigrant grandfather in 1898. Gen 2 had two of my six aunts, both of my uncles, and my father (as CEO) working in the family business. We all lived within a block of the office. Everyone worked together and dined together, and we kids (my cousins and I) played together.

From the family matriarch, Aunt Rosa, to my parents (George and Lilly Isaac), everything was a teaching moment. During my growing-up years, I regularly visited the office and also took part in dinner conversations that frequently included topics about "the business."

Upon receiving my undergraduate and MBA degrees from the University of Michigan, I surprised my family by declining employment with the family business to start my career as a management consultant with Deloitte Consulting. Consulting provided me a great introduction to managing businesses by enabling me to work with sharp colleagues on significant issues within a variety of industries.

When my Gen 2 father was ready to retire, he asked if I wanted to run the family business. My career was going great, so I declined and suggested a search for a new (nonfamily) president. After one year with the new president, the transition was not working, and the business needed new leadership. Although I was now a partner at Deloitte, I made the difficult decision to leave the firm and accept an unsolicited but urgent request from my Gen 3 cousins to be CEO of our family business. A year later, my brother, Zac, joined the business, creating a full-blown Gen 3 family business and providing me a lifelong partner and best friend.

Our generation showed our appreciation to the prior generation by growing the family's business six fold over the next eight years. We are now working on maintaining our fourth-generation business that has a larger, less connected, and more diverse ownership.

Over the past forty years, I have worked with numerous family businesses as a CEO, board member, partner and shareholder, management consultant, teacher, author, and executive mentor and coach. This book outlines the real-life lessons I have learned over the years.

I offer this work with the hope it will provide the reader with a better understanding of the tools necessary to maintain and grow a successful family business for many generations.

I organized the content by general topics, each of which offers insights and a unique perspective for addressing both the business and family issues essential for long-term success.

The chapters can be read in any order, depending upon the interests and issues facing you and your family business. The last four chapters provide nonconventional perspectives that are unique and important for managing multigenerational family enterprises: Succession Planning, Selling Your Family Business, Avoiding the Family Business Wealth Evaporation Trap, and Perpetuating Multigenerational Family Wealth.

George A. Isaac
(www.GeorgeIsaac.com)

Chapter

ONE

Family Enterprise Survival and Growth— Seven Essential Initiatives

Establish the paradigms that are critical to the ongoing success of every multigenerational family business.

FAMILY BUSINESSES FACE CONTINUAL and potentially dangerous existential threats, as do most businesses. In addition, they also bear their own unique risks associated with the transitioning of ownership and leadership from one generation to the next.

The ultimate price for failing to prepare for and meet these special challenges is *extinction*, the fate of 85 to 90 percent of family businesses after the second generation.

In planning the future of your family business, you have two strategic alternatives: maximize the company's value and sell it, or grow the firm for future generations.

In reality, selling your company today, even at maximized value, is typically a *poor financial option*.

Taxes reduce the sales proceeds. The prospective returns from reinvesting the remaining proceeds in fixed income and equity securities continue to be paltry. US long-term interest rates recently hit one of the two lowest points since 1790, and projected long-term returns on equity investments are historically low. While interest rates were recently rising as the Federal Reserve reduces its programs to stimulate the economy, overall returns for investors in fixed income are expected to remain historically low.

Prior to developing the following seven essential initiatives for managing a family business, I studied why most family businesses fail—that is, why they do not survive to the next generation. I concluded there were *business reasons* and *family reasons* that impaired multigenerational succession, often resulting in the sale or breakup among family stakeholders of the family business.

Business reasons included excessive risk acceptance, outdated business strategies, and poor management of the business. Family reasons included problematic family dynamics, inadequate succession planning, and unaligned shareholder objectives. At times, it was the deadly combination—where poor business decisions were made due to the *result of bad family dynamics*.

Without doubt, successfully growing your family business over the long term is your soundest option for navigating future economic challenges and creating (and preserving) family wealth.

To perpetuate the family business, your family leadership needs to adopt and sustain *seven critical initiatives*. Addressing these paradigms wisely will help secure your company's survival and multiply your family's future prosperity.

1. Build a Sound Governance and Ownership Foundation

Understand and *align* your family owners' goals. These are the necessary first steps to maintain a healthy family business and prepare for generational transitions. Your personal needs as owners and your company's business needs each change over time, often dramatically. Both require continual adjustment to keep your family goals on target, your ownership aligned, and your business growing.

Once goals are formulated and agreed upon, ownership must develop and codify operating and business decision-making policies. These will address issues such as majority versus super-majority voting requirements, board membership and authority levels, cash distribution policies, rules and restrictions on ownership transfers, and other ownership regulations and procedures.

A knowledgeable corporate attorney can help your family identify the issues and document your agreements in a shareholders' agreement. Depending upon the form of organization, these equity-based owner agreements are referred to as a closed corporation agreement (in C and S corporations), operating agreement (in a limited liability company, or LLC), or partnership agreement (in partnership).

See Appendix B for a detail checklist on items to address in a shareholders' agreement, the term used to refer to any equity-based owner agreements.

Once the agreement is drafted and accepted, the family's next step is to establish both a strong board of directors/advisors and a separate family council to manage governance.

The board of directors will focus on business issues, including strategies, finance, organization, business plans, succession planning, and performance oversight. Its main goal will be to represent the interests of *all* shareholders.

The family council will address the family issues that arise in every family-owned business. Its mandate will be to manage family member communications, networking and conflict resolution, family investment objectives, estate planning and ownership considerations, and direction for the board regarding family business philosophies, culture, and owner priorities.

Chapter 5 provides extensive details on developing proper family and business governance.

2. Manage Family Dynamics

Managing the family side of business is a critical task for the ownership group, often more so than the business side. Many families do not recognize its importance until irreversible damage has been done.

Most family problems occur within what I call the *Five Cs for successful family dynamics: consideration, communication, connectivity, compensation, and conflict resolution.*

Family stakeholders need to feel that their ideas are honestly considered; that they are connected to the business and kept well informed; that they are being fairly treated financially; and finally, if conflict arises, that a resolution is achieved in a timely, respectful, and professional manner.

Specific strategies and initiatives must be developed and agreed upon by family ownership for all five Cs.

Unfortunately, many CEOs and boards focus primarily or solely on the business issues and allow the people issues to take care of themselves. They believe that successful business results will overcome and resolve problematic family dynamics. They won't!

Minority ownership issues often become majority ownership's problems if not promptly resolved. Worse yet, seemingly small family dynamics problems do *not* go away over time. Rather, they simmer in the background and grow until a future trigger event raises the temperature and the issues boil over. At that stage, they are infinitely more difficult to resolve.

Chapters 3 and 4 fully discuss strategies to manage family dynamics.

3. Focus on Business Strategy

The business environment changes constantly for every business. Technology, competition, economic cycles, customer needs and desires, disruptive value propositions, government regulations, and your own financial and organizational capabilities all combine to produce a complex jigsaw puzzle for management.

A sure way to become irrelevant (and eventually nonexistent) is to assume that your existing strategies are always right. Regular review of and challenge to your strategies are essential for long-term success. SWOT analysis (looking at strengths, weaknesses, opportunities, and threats by product and market segment) is an easy way to get started.

Strategic plans should be developed by your senior management team and assessed, challenged, and approved by your board of directors. Communicating approved strategies to your stakeholders (e.g., management team, employees, key vendors, and customers) is critical to obtaining buy-in and a successful implementation. An outside facilitator often is valuable in guiding and improving the results for this planning process. He or she can help ensure that a fact-based approach is balanced and respectful of all team members' opinions in determining the appropriate business strategies.

As part of a strategic planning process, management must develop supporting business plans to determine the resource requirements, activities, and justification for implementing them. Typical business plans address a broad set of issues relating to sales and marketing, operations, technology, capital expenditures, organization and human resources, and finance.

Appendix A includes my business-planning checklist to get you started. The checklist is more exhaustive than may be required, so it can be modified for your particular strategic plan.

4. Invest in the Best Organization Affordable

Strategy defines organizational requirements.

Your goal is simple: hire the best people you can afford, put them in the right positions, evaluate them fairly, and reward them well for performance!

Top performers will pay for themselves many times over; poor performers will be very costly—well beyond their payroll cost. *Investing in people* will make all the difference in your performance.

Determining family member roles and authorities in the organization can be sticky. Those decisions *must* be based on capabilities and work ethic, not birthrights. In addition, boundaries are important, since a family employee may wear multiple hats as an owner, board member, manager, future owner, and family member.

There are many ways to have family involved and feeling "special" without compromising your management team's performance. A customized family policy manual, often titled a *family constitution*, helps establish ground rules for each family member participating in the family business, regardless of position assumed in the company.

The best organizations empower all team members. When possible, every manager and supervisor should be highly motivated and clearly authorized to run his or her piece of the business and measured against specific and agreed-upon goals. Acknowledging and rewarding outstanding performers and identifying and removing underperformers are *essential* practices of successful businesses.

Providing a good work environment is not enough! Recognition and reward systems are also critical—particularly for nonfamily executives in the business. Phantom stock plans, share appreciation rights, deferred wealth management programs, and other recognition and reward systems should be considered when developing senior management compensation plans.

5. Manage Against Metrics

What you measure and reward drives and determines your results.

Quantifiable performance metrics, developed with input from your people and aligned to support the business plan, provide a road map for success. The prerequisite is transparency in financial and operating performance measurement systems. Keep goals simple, clear, and attainable. Make performance assessment straightforward—you either accomplished your goals or you did not. Eliminate excuses for poor performance to keep your team sharply focused on meeting specific company priorities.

Publishing company-wide performance metrics throughout the organization can motivate your teams, when done appropriately. Doing so communicates goals and results and also stimulates peer pressure to perform and contribute.

As CEO of the Isaac Group, I shared production metrics and mutually agreed-upon goals for the first time with our direct line processing equipment operators. The result—our main plant doubled production without requiring any new capital expenditures.

The obvious lesson: empowering employees to focus on their individual and unit performance metrics motivates them to meet and often beat their objectives and provides a more meaningful work environment where they get to manage their piece of the business.

It is really simple. When you set goals, share information, empower your team members, and reward performance, everybody wins!

Chapter 2 addresses key questions to ask and metrics to use in evaluating your business.

6. Commit to a Culture of Growth

Any business, and particularly a family business, must grow to survive. Operating costs rise, business markets change, and product life cycles get shorter. And, as a family grows, there are more mouths to feed.

Businesses either grow and stay healthy or stagnate and die. Yes, there are lifestyle businesses that generate good cash flow despite a stagnant business model, but it is doubtful that these businesses will make it to the next generation or realize a good price if sold. Furthermore, it is difficult to recruit and retain top talent in a stagnating company.

A culture of growth *forces* a business to be competitive. It requires the business to develop new products and services, deliver a solid value proposition to customers, focus on profits and wise capital management, and sustain an entrepreneurial spirit. The result of a culture of growth is a company that generates the financial resources to reward both its people and its ownership, thus perpetuating an upward performance trajectory.

7. Cultivate an Investor Perspective

Most family owners fail to look at their business from an investor's perspective, even when the family business is their largest investment and main source of wealth. Family business leadership thus simultaneously fail to meet the changing financial needs of family members and regularly confuse the value of business returns on equity with those of *realized* shareholder returns.

Until shareholders receive cash, their returns are zero. Low levels of cash distribution result in lower shareholder realized returns, inadequate shareholder liquidity, and increased financial exposure to unforeseen "tail risks." This often results in problematic family dynamics that create major rifts within the family that can threaten the longevity of the company itself.

Look at your family owners as investors. You must run the family business to optimize *realized shareholder value and continue to address both individual and business goals* diligently to keep the ownership group satisfied and aligned.

Focus sharply on cash flow generation and distributions, in addition to profits. Measure and communicate annual changes in equity valuation, realized shareholder returns, and performance against annual business plans. Publish the results in an annual shareholder report. Carefully evaluate the business's dividend policies in light of reinvestment needs and the needs for a cash return to your shareholders. Consider partial transfer of trapped accumulated wealth in the operating businesses into newly created family investment entities. *See chapter 9 for further details.*

Employing these perspectives and actions will help you diversify your family's investment portfolio, increase asset protection and shareholder liquidity, and reduce overall risk in managing family wealth.

Utilizing these seven core initiatives also will enable you to improve your business decision-making and produce an informed and engaged ownership group that is supportive of creating an enduring, long-term, and highly successful multigenerational family business.

Chapter

TWO

Understanding and Analyzing Financial Statements

(Please scan or skip this chapter if you are financially proficient.)

Understanding financial statements is an essential skill of family members associated with a family business. Without a baseline of knowledge, you will lose either influence or money—or both!

FRUSTRATION, STRESS, CONFUSION, AND, at times, embarrassment—these are the emotions often expressed by family business clients who do not understand how to read and interpret financial statements.

Paying close attention to the signals that statements reveal and being able to understand them are the *only* ways to determine the health and vigor of a business. Developing the skills to do both is critical for any family member who is or who will be an owner or board member of a family business.

The lack of understanding financial statements is more common than many realize. A few years back, I invested in a growing computer servicing business start-up with a professional management team and independent fiduciary directors. Within eighteen months, the CEO proudly reported to his board and investors, of which I was one, that the business was breaking even.

Upon my review of the detailed financials, I noticed the financially naive CEO counted prepaid service contract cash receipts as revenues (after all, they were the result of "sales" activities, and the cash was in the bank).

I wrote to the board stating these cash receipts were not sales but liabilities, not much different than bank debt. I concluded that their business was underwater. This information was neither well received nor followed up on by the inept management team, and within six months, the bank put the company into foreclosure and eventual Chapter 7 bankruptcy—much to the surprise of the board and investor group!

My aim with this chapter is to teach the basics of understanding financial statements and to provide a reference manual so you can properly oversee your family business.

Purpose of Financial Statements

Financial statements tell a story—albeit a historical one. They report how a business has performed over a specified period of time. They show its strengths, weaknesses, ownership, risks, and financial performance and are essential for understanding any business.

At times, some owners adopt a quick and simplistic appraisal of their business's health by considering primarily the amount of cash in the bank. This measure is not only misleading, but its practice has led many businesses into unanticipated financial ruin.

An owner must pay attention to the four distinct financial documents that compose a company's financial statements:

I INCOME STATEMENT

II BALANCE SHEET

III STATEMENT OF CASH FLOW

IV STATEMENT OF CHANGES IN EQUITY

The following sections explain these four financial statements and the key questions a family owner will want to have answered about the data they provide.

Key Family Owner Questions

Five fundamental questions should be answered while reviewing business financial statements:

1. Is the company making or losing money?
2. Is the company in solid financial condition, with ample resources to meet its current obligations and future needs?
3. Is the company generating cash or consuming cash?
4. Who owns the company and in what amounts?

5. Are the owners receiving appropriate returns for the risks assumed by the business?

Just as a personal diary will cover a day or a month that has passed, financial statements specify the historical period they are reporting. For example, "fiscal year," which is often the calendar year, is any consecutive twelve-month reporting period, such as from January 1 through December 31 of a particular year. Monthly financial statements provide information on the most recent month and should also include year-to-date results for the current fiscal year.

While financial statements *do not* predict future business results, they can provide metrics and trends that are helpful in making informed projections about future results.

I. Income Statement

The income statement (or profit and loss report [P&L]) identifies the revenues and expenses that a business generates during a specific time period and whether they result in a profit or loss.

Table 1 illustrates a simple income statement organized by the typical groupings.

Starting with revenues, various costs are deducted to determine different aspects of profitability, such as *gross profit*, *operating income*, and *net income*. Each gives the reader different information about the company's performance.

Revenues recognize sales (e.g., when products are shipped or services provided) and report sales for a specified accounting period, in this case the twelve months ending December 31st.

Cost of goods sold presents the expenses incurred to produce the revenues. The goal is to match all expenses with the corresponding revenues to determine if the business is profitable. These costs include *manufacturing costs*, such as material and labor, *outbound shipping and service delivery costs*, and *plant or manufacturing overhead* costs, such as plant management salaries and benefits, building or equipment rental costs, and depreciation expenses for buildings and equipment. In a service business, it represents costs to deliver services to the client.

Table 1

Income Statement

For twelve months ending December 31, 20XX

Revenues	$20,000,000
Less: Cost of Goods Sold	(12,000,000)
Gross Profit	$8,000,000
Less: SG&A Expenses (Corporate Overhead)	(5,000,000)
Operating Income	$3,000,000
Nonoperating Items (interest income and expense, nonrecurring gains and losses)	(250,000)
Net Income before Taxes	$2,750,000
Less: Income Taxes (if paid by the corporation)	(600,000)
Net Income	$2,150,000

Depreciation expense is a noncash expense included in costs of goods sold that assigns a usage charge for an asset (e.g., plant or equipment). This cost allocates (amortizes) a portion of an asset's original cost over the duration of its expected useful life.

For example, if you bought equipment for $1 million with an expected useful life of ten years, its depreciation expense would be $100K per year ($1 million divided by ten years). In this situation, the company would have paid $1 million in Year 1 and reported expenses of $100K per year for Years 1 through 10.

The objective of depreciation is to *match,* or assign, a portion of the purchase cost for using the equipment with the associated revenues generated by the equipment to determine profit or loss.

This illustrates the importance of understanding both costs and cash flow. For example, $1 million of *cash* may have been spent to purchase the equipment in Year 1, but a depreciation *cost* of only $100K is reported in the income statement for that year and each of the following nine years.

Gross profit (or gross margin) is the first layer of analyzing profits. It is the difference between revenues less cost of goods sold.

Corporate overhead costs, also known as selling, general, and administrative costs (SG&A), are costs necessary to generate the revenues that do not relate directly to manufacturing the product or providing the service, such as executive compensation, marketing, and other corporate headquarter costs.

Operating income is the next layer of profit or loss. It is calculated by subtracting *corporate overhead (SG&A)* from gross profits. It represents the profit or loss from ongoing business operations, a key bottom-line measure.

Nonoperating items account for nonrecurring transactions. These could be a one-time gain or loss on the sale of an asset, or other nonoperating items, such as interest income and expense.

Net income before taxes represents the profit or loss after nonoperating items are included (i.e., added to or deducted from operating income).

Income taxes are reported if the *entity* pays taxes directly to the government, such as in C corporations. When this occurs, **net income** is computed by subtracting income taxes from net income before taxes.

For limited liability companies (LLCs), subchapter S corporations, and partnerships, the income is "passed through" (allocated) to the shareholders based upon each owner's percentage ownership of the business. The business income tax liability is included on the owner's individual tax returns. Therefore, income tax expenses do not show up on the business income statement, as the tax payments are made to the government directly by the owners.

Real estate companies use a slightly different income statement format but basically follow the same concepts. They start with revenues, such as rental income, and then subtract operating expenses to determine *net operating income*, or NOI (versus operating income). NOI is the main bottom line in a real estate business. It is different from operating income in that it represents both earnings and operating cash flow because it is computed before deducting depreciation, a noncash item.

Analyzing the Income Statement

The income statement and other financial statements provide additional measures of performance when analyzed using **financial metrics.**

Financial metrics are ratios expressed as percentages or per-unit figures to help the reader easily understand and compare financial and operating performance. These metrics allow a consistent comparison among multiple business units or divisions, or a comparison against such standards as industry metrics, investor objectives, and company budgets.

Financial metrics provide answers to some critical questions, such as the following:

1. Are profit margins and cost structures in line with industry or historical metrics or projected business plans?
2. Are business performance trends improving or declining?
3. Are budgets and financial plans being met?
4. Are levels of returns to shareholders adequate and acceptable?
5. Are revenues growing with acceptable profit margins?

The income statement provides specific financial data to evaluate a business, including key operating elements such as *profitability* and *costs*. These metrics are often posted in a column beside the financial numbers on the income statement.

Profitability Metrics

Similar to peeling an onion layer by layer, the common profitability metrics calculate various profitability measures as a percentage of revenues.

Common metrics include:

- Gross Margin = Gross Profits / Revenues
- Operating Margin = Operating Income / Revenues

- Net Income Margin = Net Income / Revenues
- EBITDA Margin = (Earnings Before Interest, Taxes, Depreciation, and Amortization) / Revenues

Low-margin businesses are riskier than high-margin businesses because they require a larger sales volume to pay for fixed costs. Also, low-margin businesses have a smaller profit cushion to absorb any detrimental events, such as economic downturns, increased pricing pressures from competition, or cost increases from suppliers.

Cost Structure Metrics

Understanding the *appropriateness* of the costs and how they are *changing* over time are critical to both understanding and managing the future financial performance of the business and identifying areas for improvement.

Common metrics to evaluate costs include expressing various cost elements as a

- percentage of total revenues,
- percentage of total costs,
- percent cost increase from prior year,
- percent variance from budget, and
- cost per unit (item count, hours, pounds, gallons, miles, square feet, etc.).

II. Balance Sheet

The balance sheet, also known as the statement of financial position, reports the value of a company's assets, liabilities and equity as of a specific date.

Assets are items of value that a business owns. **Liabilities** represent the amount of money that a business owes to others, including suppliers, banks, and other creditors. **Equity** represents the remaining value of the business assets that belong to the owners after subtracting all liabilities. It can be referred to as *net book value* or *book value*.

The balance sheet derives its name from the requirement that total assets must equal (balance) the sum of total liabilities and equity. The basic formula is:

ASSETS = LIABILITIES + EQUITY

The balance sheet, depicted in table 2, is organized around these three categories. In partnerships, equity might be referred to as "partner capital."

Assets

There are two types of assets: current and noncurrent.

Current assets represent assets that are in the form of cash, or assets that are expected to be converted into cash within twelve months of the statement date. They consist of cash, accounts receivable (payments due from customers), inventories (raw materials, work-in-process, and finished goods), and prepaid expenses (expenses to be realized or incurred at a later date but already paid for).

Table 2

Balance Sheet

As of December 31, 20XX

ASSETS	LIABILITIES
Current Assets:	**Current Liabilities:**
Cash and Equivalents	Accounts Payable
Accounts Receivable	Accrued Expenses
Inventories	Unearned Revenue
Prepaid Expenses	Notes Payable
Total Current Assets	Total Current Liabilities
Noncurrent Assets:	**Long Term Liabilities:**
Land	Notes Payable
Plant and Equipment	Total Long Term Liabilities
Accumulated Depreciation	**Total Liabilities**
Intangibles and Goodwill	**Equities**
Total Noncurrent Assets	Common Stock or Capital Accounts
Total Assets	Preferred Stock
TOTAL ASSETS = TOTAL LIABILITIES + EQUITY	Retained Earnings
	Total Equity
	TOTAL LIABILITIES and EQUITY

Noncurrent assets are longer-term assets that are not expected to be converted into cash within the next twelve months. They include land, plant and equipment less depreciation, and intangibles and goodwill. Land is recorded at its original purchase cost. Plant and equipment is also recorded at original cost but is depreciated or reduced in value each year to reflect usage over its expected life.

Intangibles and goodwill are items that are purchased but do not have physical assets associated with them. Examples include intellectual property (e.g., patents) or the portion of the cost of an acquisition that is greater than the fair market valuation of the assets acquired.

Noncurrent asset values are not reflective of current market values, as the assets are recorded at original cost. They often have increased in value over the time elapsed since their purchase date (e.g., real estate).

Liabilities

Liabilities are the company's obligations to others. Liabilities reduce the value of the equity in the business. Like a house mortgage, the value of the house must be reduced by any outstanding mortgage loans to determine the owner's equity value.

Liabilities are also divided into current (payable within twelve months) and long term (payable later than twelve months).

Current liabilities are composed of accounts payable (payments due to suppliers and vendors), accrued expenses (unpaid but incurred operating expenses due to others, such as payroll or taxes), unearned revenues (customer deposits for future services or product), and notes payable (short-term debt due to others, often a bank).

Long-term liabilities are bank and other permanent financings that are not due within the next twelve months. Real estate mortgages, longer-term bank debt, and other commercial borrowings are included in this category. When a portion of long-term debt is due to be paid within twelve months, that payment portion of the liability is transferred to the current liability "notes payable" section.

Owners' Equity, Equity, or Partner Capital Accounts

The equity value of a company is equal to assets less liabilities. It can be positive or negative (e.g., if there were sustained operating losses).

Equity represents the owners' *net book value* of the business, because it is based primarily on original asset purchase prices without any adjustments to current market value. As a result, mature companies can have a book value for equity significantly lower than fair market value. It is not, therefore, a meaningful measure of the owners' current value in the business.

Some companies may produce a "market value" balance sheet to provide additional insights on values, particularly when asset-based borrowings are contemplated (e.g., a mortgage loan on a company warehouse). A market value balance sheet is not recognized as a generally accepted accounting practice for financial reporting.

The main components of equity or owners' equity are *common shareholders*, *preferred shareholders*, and *retained earnings*. Common shareholders include *common stockholders* (in C or S corporations) and *membership or partnership interests* (in limited liability companies or partnerships).

Common shareholders participate in the governance of the business by electing a board of directors. They are directly impacted by positive or negative changes to the value of the business.

At times, **preferred stock** is used for special situations when additional capital is required for the business. Preferred stock is a separate class of stock, which typically has defined dividends and is less impacted by changes in the value of the business. Accordingly, preferred shareholders generally have fewer voting rights and less control over business decisions but have a priority distribution of income before distributions to common shareholders.

Retained earnings represent the cumulative profits and losses of the business, less any cumulative distributions or dividends paid to the owners.

Analyzing the Balance Sheet

Examining the balance sheet is critical for assessing the risks and investment returns of the business.

Owners and management should focus on addressing three fundamental areas:

1. Liquidity and Solvency

- Does the company have ample cash on hand to meet its immediate obligations?

- Does the company have the financial resources to meet future liabilities due within the next twelve months (e.g., cash to pay off loans, fund payroll, pay suppliers, purchase capital equipment, and meet fixed costs, such as building rent)?

2. Capital Structure and Risk

- Does the business have a sufficient amount of equity to meet unexpected contingencies or to weather economic storms?

- Does the company have an ability to generate additional cash through borrowing or conversion of assets into cash, if necessary, to meet longer-term obligations?

- Is there an appropriate balance between equity and debt capital or is the business overleveraged and risky (i.e., too much debt)?

3. Ownership Returns

- Are the returns on investors' capital appropriate for the amount of capital invested in the business?

- Are the returns on investors' capital reasonable for the risk being assumed by the business?

- Are the returns meeting projections provided by management?

Liquidity and Solvency Metrics

Working capital is the lifeblood of any business. It is a critical and existential item to analyze to determine the health of a business. Working capital provides the cash to meet short-term obligations. Companies go bankrupt from running out of cash, regardless of their profitability.

Cash is consumed and generated throughout the business cycle and impacts working capital accounts (current assets and current liabilities) as follows:

- *Accounts receivable (a current asset)*: Cash is generated when customers pay the company for their purchases. If customers do not pay at time of delivery, the amount they owe is added to accounts receivable. When paid, accounts receivable is decreased.

- *Accounts payable (a current liability)*: Cash is consumed or spent when a company pays its suppliers for materials and other operating costs to produce its product or service. If these costs are not paid at time of purchase, the amount owed is added to accounts payable. When payments are made by the company, accounts payable is decreased.

- *Inventory (a current asset)*: This captures the costs to produce a company's product or service, and until the product is sold, the costs are added to inventory. When the product is sold, the costs are reduced (i.e., removed) from inventory.

Working capital is computed by subtracting current liabilities from current assets. It compares the current assets in the business (assets that are cash or should turn into cash over the next twelve months) with the current liabilities (obligations that will need to be paid over the same time period).

The goal is to have significantly greater current assets than current liabilities so that there is a cushion of liquidity (i.e., cash or assets easily convertible to cash) to meet all of the obligations of the business. Two key metrics to evaluate working capital are as follows:

- Current Ratio = Current Assets / Current Liabilities
- Quick Ratio = (Cash + Marketable Securities + Receivables) / Current Liabilities

A good rule of thumb is to maintain a current ratio equal to or greater than 2.0 and a quick ratio equal to or greater than 1.0.

That would provide twice the value of current assets to pay for current liabilities and at least 100 percent coverage of current liabilities without the sale of existing inventories.

The major subcomponents of working capital are *accounts receivable*, *inventory*, and *accounts payable*. To gain a proper understanding of the condition of the business, owners must analyze each of these subcomponents of working capital.

For example, suppose the current assets were significantly larger than the current liabilities. One could conclude that liquidity is fine. If, however, upon closer examination it was revealed that over 50 percent of the accounts receivable were over sixty days past due, this information might justify reversing the initial conclusion. It could, for example, identify a major problem with the *collectability* of customer accounts receivables, a possibility that requires deeper investigation.

The following metrics evaluate the subcomponents of working capital:

- Accounts Receivable Days Outstanding = Accounts Receivable / Average Daily Revenues

  This metric is an indicator of whether A/R is composed of current or past-due transactions. If it shows an excessive number of days outstanding over the terms of sale, management should require an accounts receivable aging report to identify accounts receivable by age, usually in thirty-day past-due increments. Past-due receivables could represent uncollectible balances that should have been written off (i.e., expensed).

- Inventory Days = Inventory / Average Daily Cost of Goods Sold

  This measurement estimates the number of days' supply of inventory in stock. A large number can indicate slow-moving or obsolete inventory, which may not be worth its stated value on the balance sheet.

- Accounts Payable Days = Accounts Payable / Average Daily Cost of Goods Sold

  This measurement reveals how quickly the business is paying its vendor. Ideally, the business is paying per the terms of purchase. When this metric is high (greater than sixty days), it suggests the company may have financial liquidity problems.

  Note: Calculating average daily revenues and average cost of goods sold (COGS) based upon the prior two months is better than using annual numbers, particularly in cyclical businesses. This information is found in the income statement.

Capital Structure and Risk Metrics

Highly leveraged companies have a large portion of their capital base in debt, not equity. While returns to equity owners are enhanced by increasing leverage through additional debt, this strategy creates a riskier business. Such businesses can get into financial trouble during a downturn when they are not able to make debt service payments on time or at all.

Companies with minimal or no debt have less risk but also provide lower returns to the equity owners. Thus, owners should help determine the "sweet spot" (i.e., the appropriate level of risk and financial leverage) for the business to meet ownership risk-return objectives.

Two metrics to evaluate the capital structure of a business in terms of leverage are as follows:

- Debt to Equity Ratio = Total Liabilities / Total Equity
- Debt to Assets Ratio = Total Liabilities / Total Assets

  Note: Many variations are used in defining total liabilities. My preference is to include all interest-bearing debt, which would exclude accounts payables and other non-interest-bearing liabilities.

A good way to evaluate leverage is to determine if the company has ample recurring *cash flow* to meet debt payment requirements. The main metric is the measure of excess cash flow available to meet required payments for debt service and other fixed costs, such as rent. These are two commonly used metrics:

- Debt Service Ratio = EBITDA* / Debt Service Payments**

  *Or in a real estate company, Net Operating Income / Debt Service Payments***

  **EBITDA is earning before interest, taxes, depreciation, and amortization, similar to operating income plus depreciation.*

  ***Includes principal and interest payments.*

- Fixed Charge*** Coverage Ratio = (EBITDA + Fixed Charges) / Fixed Charges

  ****Fixed charges include debt service payments and other fixed expenditures, such as lease payments due within twelve months.*

Ownership Returns Metrics

Typically, high-growth companies retain earnings to provide capital for future business growth. Low-growth companies that cannot put additional capital to good use should not retain earnings (so long as their working capital is adequate). Otherwise, owners receive a lower investment return on their retained capital. The better approach is to distribute the earning to the owners and allow them to invest their money in other assets that may produce better returns.

Return expectations should be balanced with the ownership's approved risk profile of the business—higher risk should deliver higher returns. Metrics to measure investor returns include the following:

- Return on Assets = Net Income / Average Total Assets
- Return on Equity = Net Income / Average Equity
- Return on Capital Employed = Net Income / (Average of Total Long-Term Debt + Equity)

Averages are computed on either monthly balances or the beginning and ending year-end balances. Net income information is provided in the income statement, while the other information is provided in the balance sheet.

III. Statement of Cash Flow

Cash flow is the net amount of cash and cash-equivalents (e.g., money market funds, treasury bills) being transferred into and out of a business during the statement period.

Cash flow is different from profits. Both need to be carefully measured and managed. The *statement of cash flow* reports if a company is generating or consuming cash.

Three primary areas impact cash flow: (1) operating activities, (2) investing activities, and (3) financing activities. The difference in the cash balances from the beginning to the end of the reporting period is cash flow. Table 3 illustrates a typical statement of cash flow.

Cash flow from operating activities is determined from the cash generated or consumed in the income statement's profits or losses and the balance sheet changes in working capital.

Noncash expenses, such depreciation and amortization, are subtracted when computing net income on the income statement. Therefore, these costs must be added back to net income to

Table 3

Statement Of Cash Flow

For twelve months ending December 31, 20XX

Cash Flow From Operating Activities:

+ Net Income

+ Depreciation and Amortization

+/- Decrease in Accounts Receivable

+/- Decrease in Inventories

+/- Decrease in Prepaid Expenses

+/- Increase in Accounts Payable

+/- Increase in Accrued Expenses

Net Cash Flow From Operating Activities (A)

Cash Flow From Investing Activities:

+ Sale of Fixed Assets (e.g., facilities or equipment)

- Purchase of Fixed Assets (capital expenditures)

Net Cash Flow From Investing Activities (B)

Cash Flow From Financing Activities:

- Principal Payments on Notes

+ Borrowing of New Funds

- Payment of distributions or dividends to owners

+/- Refinancing of Debt

Net Cash Flow From Financing Activities (C)

Net Cash Flow (A+B+C)

Beginning Cash Balance

Ending Cash Balance

determine cash flow from operating activities. Additional adjustments are made based upon changes in working capital accounts to reflect the actual cash received (e.g., changes in accounts receivables) and the actual cash paid for operating expenses (e.g., changes in accounts payables).

Cash flow from investing activities reports the cash generated from the sale of fixed assets or consumed from the acquisition of fixed assets (e.g., plant, property, and equipment). This section assumes the transactions were cash based.

Cash flow from financing activities reports the cash generated from the issuance of new debt or refinancing of existing debt and the cash consumed from the payment of principal on existing debt. It also reports cash distributions or dividends to owners.

The cash flow sections are interrelated for certain types of transactions. For example, if an equipment acquisition reported in the investing section was financed with debt, then the issuance of debt would be displayed in the financing section. The net impact on cash flow would be the difference between the acquisition cost of the equipment less the amount of debt used to pay for it.

The net cash flow of the business over the accounting period is the summation of these three sections of cash flow. A *positive* net cash flow results when cash is generated and a *negative* cash flow when cash is consumed. The result is more or less cash in the business.

Analyzing the Statement of Cash Flow

The statement of cash flow reveals if the company is generating cash and, if it is, whether it results from operations or from increased borrowings. For long-term viability, cash needs to be generated from profitable operations, not from financing activities. If a company is reporting profits but losing cash over time, there may be problems that need to be resolved.

Analyzing the statement of cash flow should answer the following questions:

1. Is the business generating cash flows commensurate with its profitability?

2. Is the company generating cash from operations or from increased borrowings?

3. Is the business reinvesting cash into future cash generating assets, as evidenced by investments in capital equipment?

4. Are owner cash distributions appropriate given business conditions and the company's ability to continue generating cash flow?

Cash Flow Metrics

Important cash flow metrics include the following:

- Operating Cash Flow Margin = Cash Flow from Operating Activities / Revenues

- Capital Expenditure Reinvestment Rate = Capital Expenditures / Depreciation Expense

- Dividend Payout Ratio = Dividends or Distributions / Net Income

IV. Statement of Changes in Equity

The statement of changes in equity reports all changes to the owners' equity or partnership capital accounts. Its purpose is to provide transparency on capital account transactions during a reporting period. Since equity is what the shareholders or owners of a company actually own, it is important to disclose any changes in equity because they are *not* displayed in the other financial statements.

As an example, if new shares in the company were sold to another party, the current owners would want to be aware of this action, as it would directly impact their percentage ownership in the business. Most likely, shareholder or partnership agreements would dictate the process for issuing new ownership units. Nonetheless, observing and understanding the financial impact of equity transactions is important for every family owner.

Table 4 illustrates a basic statement of changes in equity. Starting with opening balances, the report details transactions impacting owners' equity throughout the year.

In this illustration, the opening balances show $10 million in total owners' equity. It is composed of $1 million in contributed equity from the prior sale of stock or ownership interests. It also includes a beginning balance of $9 million in retained earnings, representing the cumulative amount of annual net income that had been retained to date.

Table 4

Statement of Changes in Equity

For twelve months ending December 31, 20XX

	EQUITY ACCOUNT	RETAINED EARNINGS	TOTAL OWNERS' EQUITY
Balance as of January 1, 20XX	$1,000,000	$9,000,000	$10,000,000
Issuance of new equity	$150,000		$150,000
Redemption of existing equity	($50,000)		($50,000)
Current year net income		$2,150,000	$2,150,000
Dividends and distributions		($1,000,000)	($1,000,000)
Other equity transactions			
Ending balance as of December 31, 20XX	$1,100,000	$10,150,000	$11,250,000

In the equity column, the statement reports $150,000 in new equity (i.e., stock or ownership interests) sold and $50,000 in equity purchased by the company from existing owners. The retained earnings column reports current net income of $2,150,000 (from the income statement), of which $1,000,000 (from the statement of cash flow) was distributed to the owners.

Communicating Financial Information

Senior family business leaders often struggle to determine the best way to communicate financial information to family owners who may possess varying proficiencies in reading and understanding financial statements. Using visual presentations that help illuminate trends, such as charts and graphs, are an excellent approach for both board member presentations and family reporting. As they say, a picture is worth a thousand words! In addition, some people are more naturally inclined to visual learning than others.

The following sample charts and graphs could be helpful as a starting point for developing your family business reporting packet. The metrics and details can vary based on your specific company's key metrics and areas of focus.

I utilized similar trend graphs and charts for our Isaac board meetings, and they were well received. I also found them helpful for our management retreats.

These basic questions should be addressed in family shareholder reporting:

- Is the business making money and performing well?
- Is it in good financial condition with adequate funds to pay its bills and reinvest in the business?
- Are the shareholders receiving acceptable returns on their investment?
- Are the trends improving or declining?

A one-pager summarizing key metrics on operating results, working capital management, and capital structure is a good starting point. The following table 5 is an example—it is simple, covers the basics, is easy to understand, and is highly informative.

Table 5

Financial Performance Summary

For twelve months ending December 31, 20XX

	SAMPLE FINANCIAL METRICS				
Metric	**Current Year**		**Budget or Prior Year**		
	#	**%**	**#**	**%**	**Variance**
Operating Metrics					
Revenues	$45,500,000	100%	$50,000,000	100%	$(4,500,000)
Cost of Sales	$29,575,000	65.0%	$33,000,000	66.0%	$(3,425,000)
Gross Profit	$15,925,000	35.0%	$17,000,000	34.0%	$(1,075,000)
S.G. & A	$10,237,500	22.5%	$10,000,000	20.0%	$(237,500)
Operating Profit	$5,687,500	12.5%	$7,000,000	14.0%	$(1,312,500)
Net Income	$5,232,500	11.5%	$6,500,000	13.0%	$(1,267,500)
Working Capital Metrics					
Working Capital	$6,500,000		$7,500,000		$(1,000,000)
Current Ratio	2.3		2.5		-0.2
Quick Ratio	1.2		1.3		-0.1
A/R Days Outstanding	45		42		3
Inventory Days Supply	42		38		4
A/P Days Outstanding	35		35		0
Capital Structure Metrics					
Debt Service Ratio	1.65		1.75		(0.10)
Return on Capital	14.5%		18.0%		-3.5%
Return on Equity	16.1%		20.0%		-3.9%

Graphs display trends vividly. They also are easy to read and remember.

Graphs 1 and 2 show whether revenues are growing and producing acceptable profit margins. As a reminder, gross profits are revenues less cost of goods sold (including both variable and fixed manufacturing costs of goods sold).

Graph 1. Revenue and Gross Profit Margin Trends

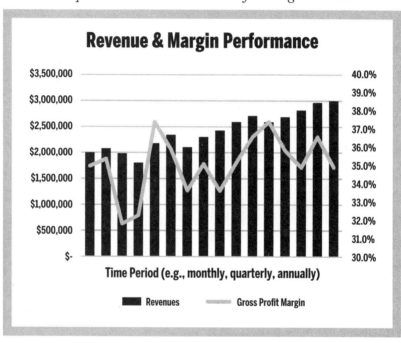

Graph 2 introduces an additional profit margin calculation, *variable contribution margin (*the difference between revenues and variable cost of goods sold). It is useful in determining a company's break-even revenue point and in pricing decisions to be certain the business is not losing money on incremental sales. Revenues in excess of variable costs "pay for" fixed manufacturing costs and corporate overhead (SG&A) with any excess producing operating profits.

Graph 2. Profitability Trends Percentage of Revenues

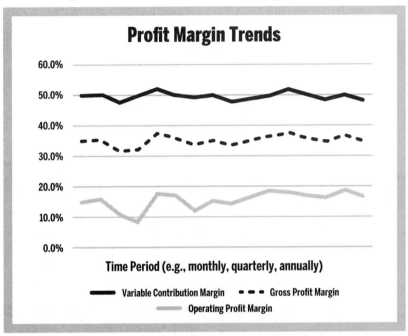

Cost management is another key metric that needs to be reported, particularly if profit margins are disappointing.

Graph 3 addresses manufacturing cost trends with an emphasis on cost per unit manufactured.

Graph 4 examines corporate overhead (SG&A) with an emphasis on overhead cost as a percentage of revenue.

Graph 5 provides a breakdown of business revenues by cost category and profit.

Graph 3. Manufacturing Cost Trends

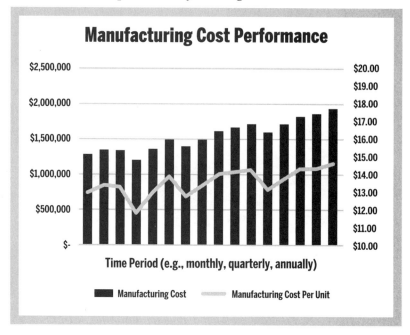

Graph 4. Corporate Overhead Cost Trends

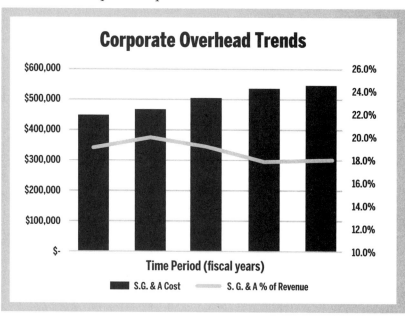

Graph 5. Business Cost Structure

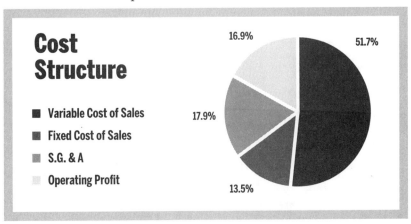

Understanding where profits are generated and losses are produced is an important management focus. Simple pie charts can be an excellent way to depict this information by various segments—product lines, distribution channels, geographic territories, manufacturing plants, etc. These can be easily displayed as illustrated in graph 6.

Graph 6. Sample Profit Contributions By Sector

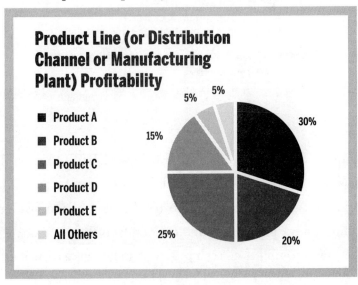

Managing working capital is critical to ensure that any business has enough cash to operate. Loss of cash due to uncollectible accounts receivable, write-offs from obsolete inventories, or loss of suppliers due to poor payment practices must be carefully monitored.

Graph 7 captures the three key metrics to monitor working capital in your business.

Graph 7. Working Capital Metrics

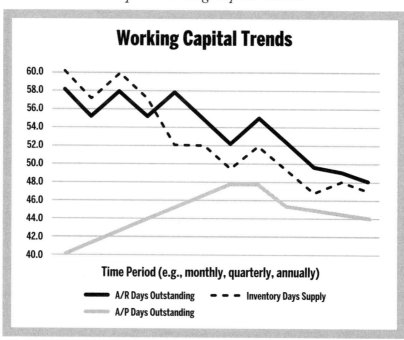

Graph 8 displays the pretax cash flow (EBITDA) trends of the business over time. Cash is needed for capital expenditures, retention of earnings, tax payments (or distributions to owners for pass-through tax payments), and dividends to shareholders.

This graph combines all cash paid to shareholders as distributions, regardless of whether it represents funds for tax obligations or dividends. An alternative approach is to separate cash distributions for tax liabilities from distributions of earnings (dividends).

An additional metric displayed is the percentage of company cash flow that is actually distributed to the shareholders. This is often a very important metric for shareholders not employed in the family business.

Graph 8. Ownership Cash Distributions

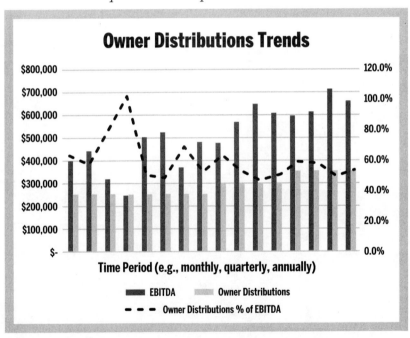

Summary

Understanding financial statements is important for every owner in order to determine the health of the business and the value of the owner's investment.

This chapter outlines several metrics that should be computed and reported as part of the best practices for evaluating a business. Owners should *insist* that their management team prepares these metrics and includes them in their regularly published financial statements.

As part of good financial management, owners and key managers should also receive an annual budget with target metrics. Reporting should compare actual results against budgeted numbers, with a written analysis explaining major variances. When business conditions or business outlooks change, revised forecasts or new projections should be prepared to provide transparency regarding management's assessment of the changes and their best estimate of future performance.

Chapter

THREE

Family Dynamics—The Forces That Build or Destroy Your Family Enterprise

Learn how family dynamics can destroy your family enterprise and the best practices that can prevent such a failure.

PICTURE THIS: YOU ARE a tremendous business success! You have created a successful enterprise and established a family enterprise to provide financial support, employment opportunities, and a mission for your present and future generations. Everything seems to have worked out. However, at some point, the family part of the family enterprise begins to disintegrate, harming the business along with the family relationships.

Holding together a multigeneration family enterprise is difficult. The core legacy and natural focal point, the original family business, may no longer be meaningful to future generations who are not involved with the business. Eventually, problems related to such disassociation cause many family enterprises to end.

What makes this scenario tragic is that many of the increasingly contentious family dynamics that threaten the longevity of the family enterprise could have been resolved. The untangling of complicated family dynamics simply requires addressing on a timely basis the "people issues" associated with family stakeholders. Unfortunately, such considerations are often overlooked by senior family members, deferred by succeeding generations, and ignored by family enterprise boards.

Needs-Based Differences

Any approach to managing family dynamics must recognize that the priorities, interests, and needs of family members are not only diverse but also ever changing. Factors such as age, marital status, lifestyle, health, income, risk tolerances, and life goals are likely to transform over time. When interests do not align or are not acknowledged and respected *at any stage* of a business's history, a potential flashpoint arises for family conflict that can endanger the enterprise's continuing existence.

The challenges are magnified with each succeeding generation as families are extended and new members are added. Instead of dealing with siblings, family management now might be dealing with first-, second-, or third-generation cousins or new spouses, any of whose family ties might be less tight.

When the fundamental reason for being part of a family enterprise is weakened or lost, the experience then transitions to one that is impersonal. In a short time, it can devolve to a purely negative financial view, namely that the family enterprise is a constraint on access to inherited assets or an obstacle to liquidity. This can lead to serious adversarial relationships.

Families then do not speak to each other because of perceived or real slights. They skip holidays, weddings, and other milestones because of family enterprise–related tensions. Underlying frictions rise to the surface, most commonly when the prior generation becomes disengaged from the family enterprise and personal agendas are pursued by their succeeding generation.

Avoiding these unhappy, painful, and potentially costly events requires acknowledging, facing, and resolving the relevant issues. This is easier to handle *while* the prior generation is still actively engaged in family affairs.

I recently helped a client work with her children and their spouses to define and secure each family member's needs and desires. Thoughtful communication was necessary to resolve the family members' emotional and financial needs while still preserving the family enterprise's future viability.

The result for my client was the development of agreed-upon written plans (owners' agreement, employment agreements, and updated estate plans) to address current needs and desires of both passive and active stakeholders *and* a methodology and governance structure to address future issues.

It is critically important for each family member to understand and respect the needs of fellow stakeholders at an *individual* level so that an overall structure can be developed that meets individual as well as enterprise needs.

Defining Family Member Roles

A major contributor to problematic family dynamics is family members themselves, who often do not have a good understanding of their various roles.

An important initial step toward increasing their understanding is to ensure that all family members are cognizant of certain realities regarding their rights and responsibilities in the various roles they play in the family and the family enterprise. The difficulty stems from defining their appropriate role in different situations. Too many believe that *being an owner* provides them with rights and a strong voice on *everything* associated with the business.

In 1978, Renato Tagiuri and John Davis of Harvard Business School developed a Venn diagram to help family members thoroughly understand their various roles and ground rules that each has in a family enterprise. Their following three-circle model depicts the seven potential roles associated with family enterprises. The model differentiates family, management/employee, and ownership-based potential roles.

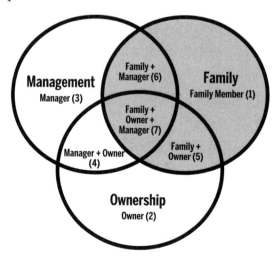

As one quickly sees, there are four distinct roles a family member can play:

- A family member is neither employed by the enterprise nor an owner. However, this family member may be a future owner. He or she probably feels connected to the family enterprise and is likely a relative of one of the family member owners (1).

- A family member is an owner but is not employed by the enterprise (5).

- A family member is employed by the enterprise and is not an owner but has the potential to become an owner (6).

- A family member is an owner and is employed by the enterprise (7).

Problems occur because family member roles and organizational boundaries are neither understood, followed, nor respected.

My colleague, Lee Hausner, PhD, a faculty member of the Family Business Program at USC's Marshall School of Business, writes about this issue in her book, *Hats Off to You 2* (coauthored with Ernest A. Doud, Jr.). Family members, she says, need to understand what "hat" they should be wearing for the differing roles they may have in the business.

A common conflicting role is an underperforming son reporting to his CEO father. Father is the boss but also the dad. Navigating through these complexities is one of the challenges of family enterprises and requires strong interpersonal skills on the part of the leaders to help family members exercise their roles appropriately and positively.

For example, does the family owner not employed by the business have the right to go into the office and start instructing management on what to do or even express his or her frustrations to management? No—he or she needs to work through proper channels, most likely the board of directors that represents the owners, or perhaps informally with the CEO.

Now let's assume a family owner is on the board of directors. Does that give him or her the right to give directions to the CEO? Again, the answer is no. A single director has no authority as an individual other than voting on issues at board meetings. Control and power reside solely with the board, the authoritative *organization* that provides direction to the CEO (through its board resolutions).

The recognition of which *hat* a family member is wearing at any time is difficult for many to understand or perceive. Regardless, all family members share the common goal of wanting success for the enterprise.

Frequent problems occur when family owners in management positions make controversial but necessary business decisions. For example, a family member with 40 percent ownership of the company may disagree with the CEO, who has 20 percent. Does that 40 percent family member have more influence and final decision-making approval than the CEO, who made the decision but only has a 20 percent ownership? The answer is unequivocally no!

Unfortunately, too often the 40 percent owner thinks he or she has or should have more authority to make the final decision. Such decisions must be made by the CEO and ratified by the board. If this process is not honored, major conflict can occur, along with disruption to the management organization.

This topic is especially challenging for family members who are not accustomed to working in a business organization or who are more wedded to the prior generation's process based upon voting by all family owners. In today's business world, management must be responsible and accountable to the board, thus requiring effective organizational structures to be followed.

The solution to these role issues is education for all family members. Family harmony and goodwill is important to the success of the business. The issue is ever present, and family conflict in the enterprise can quickly spill over to family conflict outside the enterprise, again endangering the enterprise.

In the next chapter, we will discuss specific organizational and structural strategies to prevent problematic family dynamics.

Road Map for Success

The core areas of family dynamic difficulties center around the following elements:

- Mutual respect
- Family inclusiveness
- Power and control
- Perceived fairness
- Compensation

Family enterprises can focus on their issues and resolutions by concentrating on these five Cs for success: **consideration, communication, connectivity, compensation, and conflict resolution.**

Consideration of family members' emotional and financial needs sounds obvious, but it is truly thorny and thus rarely addressed in any measurable way. Consideration, above all other elements, provides the foundation for positive dynamics in a family enterprise.

The first step is defining the family's *collective* values regarding the enterprise. Family history is a powerful starting point for establishing a sense of commonality of interest. Begin with a few basic questions:

- What are the values we all share and trust?
- Why was the original business started?
- Why do we have a family business today?
- How do we balance family needs with the enterprise's needs?

As one might imagine, reconciling the needs and desires of various passive family members can be a contentious issue. Resolution requires clear identification and agreement on the various roles and responsibilities for both the active and the passive family members, whether as an owner, a member of a family council or the company board, an employee, or a future stakeholder.

Communication is also critical—not only *what* you communicate but *how* you communicate. Interpersonal communications skills are one of the biggest challenges for family members speaking with their generational peers.

Don't treat your kid brother like you did when you both were growing up! Communication is also problematic between parents and children. While there is always a parent-child relationship, the workplace requires a different relationship between coworkers or boss and subordinate. Remember, your choice of words and style of communication matter—often more than the message!

The creation and utilization of two widely accepted governance structures, the family council and the board of directors, are extremely helpful in creating bodies that develop strategy for clear and consistent communication on family and business issues. They are central because they provide *participative* governance of a family enterprise.

As a former third-generation family business CEO, I advise my clients to communicate regularly and meaningfully with all family owners and include individualized updates to all key stakeholders, whenever possible.

Verbal communications from the family business CEO or head of the family, along with supporting written reports, are much more effective than merely published quarterly or annual reports. Some family members may not read or understand the content of a report, or it may be inconvenient or difficult for them to get answers to questions that arise and are important to them.

Part of the value of the communication is recognizing, respecting, and acknowledging all family stakeholders as sufficiently important that the company leaders are willing to take time to discuss family affairs with them. Good communication with family members and open access to information help flush out concerns before they become magnified and antagonistic. Furthermore, they help keep the family unified in pursuing common and individual goals that collectively meet the needs of all family members.

In today's connected world, there are no excuses for inadequate communication with key family members and other stakeholders. Tools such as video calling via Skype or similar software, private family websites, Facebook private discussion boards, and so on make personalized pseudo "in-person" communication accessible with family members in all corners of the globe. Use these tools to prevent family dynamic problems due to lack of communication. They also can address the next C—connectivity.

Connectivity among all family constituents is essential to creating both a sense of purpose and a personal identity with the family and the family enterprise. In addition, shared educational, philanthropic, financial and investment, and social agendas are all fundamental activities that help hold a family together for multiple generations.

Annual family gatherings are valuable events for developing and sustaining personal relationships. They allow future generations to meet each other regularly, provide a venue for training about the purpose of the family enterprise, and enable sharing of the family history. All of this contributes to a sense of connectedness and common purpose. Leaders who consciously promote meaningful connectedness significantly increase the odds that future generations of family members will see the purpose and benefits of working together to maintain the family enterprise.

Compensation for family stakeholders is a critical issue that *must* be addressed—and thoughtfully. Cash and other benefits are often a hidden problem, a major aspect of family dynamics that speaks to issues of fairness and equity among family members. Fairness is a difficult judgment, as it is based on individual perspectives and the different needs, desires, and contributions of various family members. Wisdom and care are necessary in the ongoing task of maintaining prudent family business practices while meeting the expressed needs of active and passive stakeholders.

Discussions must consider overall family enterprise financial resources and capital needs, appropriate compensation and perks for family employees, and individual shareholder needs relative to distributions. Bringing sensitivity and objectivity to these discussions is essential. Once discussed in a respectful and inclusive way, an owners' operating agreement and employment agreements that legally memorialize these and other important stakeholder issues can be negotiated and agreed upon.

Conflict resolution is an essential component for preventing problematic family dynamics from evolving into a major dispute at a family enterprise. Both informal and formal processes need to be established and agreed upon by family stakeholders in order for the family to be prepared to address future conflicts as they surface. This process is usually designed and managed by the family council.

When I am involved with a client at this stage, I prefer a three-phased approach to designing a conflict resolution process that utilizes the *prevention*, *detection*, and *resolution* strategies that are discussed in the following chapter.

Developing Passive Stakeholder Strategies

Passive stakeholders frequently have a minimal voice in the management of a family enterprise. They often feel "trapped," with no control and no meaningful options to get out. This dangerous situation can lead to lawsuits, disruption of operations, embarrassing public relations, and overall poor family dynamics. Such circumstances often set enterprise interests against personal ones. These are some best-practice passive stakeholder strategies that I have developed for my clients who face these issues:

- Developing a binding owners' operating agreement that addresses policy issues such as individual shareholder rights, key decision-making authorities, shareholder distribution policies, and governance issues, among others;
- Electing passive stakeholder(s) to the board of directors (in addition to the family council);
- Naming a passive stakeholder as the board chair to provide more balance and communication between active and passive shareholders in decision-making and agenda-setting processes;
- Providing board meeting attendance rights for non-board members (apart from executive sessions);
- Inviting passive stakeholders to enterprise outings, special events, award ceremonies, retirement parties, and extended family social events and perks;

- Providing regular financial reports, business plans, and other stakeholder communications to passive stakeholders;

- Avoiding the discussion of business at family outings; or if this occurs, including passive family members in the discussion;

- Avoiding any action that makes family members feel like a "second-class" participant in the business or the family.

Understanding and addressing the differing needs of all family stakeholders, clearly delineating duties and responsibilities, promoting transparent and regular communication policies, developing and executing an agreed-upon owners' operating agreement for all stakeholders, and creating a vehicle for long-term conflict resolution will support positive family dynamics and foster a successful family enterprise for generations to come.

Chapter

FOUR

Preventing and Managing Family Conflict

*Understand and utilize the strategies necessary to keep family
dynamics from endangering the survival of your family enterprise.*

I HAVE WITNESSED FIRSTHAND how easily family dynamics can
destroy a once-thriving family enterprise. In fact, intrafamily problems and conflicting personal objectives are a major reason why
family enterprises do not survive.

While family conflict can be a problem, it is not necessarily
unusual or unhealthy. We all understand that whenever there is
more than one person impacted by a decision, conflict may result,
regardless of the ownership or structure of an organization. Conflict
is a normal part of the management process.

Indeed, conflict often leads to better decision making, if handled
appropriately.

When conflict in family enterprises arises, it introduces potentially strong family-centric emotions and drama that can impact the business environment and will continue to resonate and reignite in home discussions. ("Why does your brother or cousin always get more than we do?"). It is this 24/7 aspect of family conflict that can erode long-standing family relationships and threaten the business.

At their worst, such negative family dynamics can tear families apart or take them into expensive and acrimonious legal actions, which rarely have a winner. The end result is often the sale of the business and the loss of significant value.

As one might expect, each succeeding generation has increasing challenges in getting along. For example, the business owners beginning in Gen 3 have been raised by different parents and often have different values and family cultures. They may live in different parts of the country or even abroad.

Over time, more and more owners lose the tight connection to the family enterprise of their prior generations, who often were employed by the company or served on the board. Family identity is weakened or even lost. The family starts viewing the business as a distant cash-generating machine controlled by others. Add historical family baggage to the mix and the challenges can become immense and emotionally charged.

In these situations, the root cause of the conflict can be difficult to diagnose. In fact, issues can surface (and incubate) from experiences occurring several years before or even from those taking place within the family and outside of the family enterprise.

Preventing Problematic Family Dynamics from Destroying a Family Enterprise

The simplest and most effective strategy is to *acknowledge and anticipate* family dynamics problems and then take steps to *prevent* them from gestating.

Many proactive actions can prevent family conflicts from arising and festering, particularly when taken during or in advance of a transition from one generation to the next. Given that one cannot always *prevent* family conflicts, early *detection* is essential to nip them in the bud before they can grow and become destructive.

Critical and most difficult is the final step, the one that *resolves* the identified conflict in the least offensive and most cost-effective manner. This is done through the development of an agreed-upon *conflict resolution process*.

A three-phase strategy—**prevention, detection, and resolution**—works, but it requires the full involvement and commitment of all family stakeholders.

Too often, family leaders mistakenly believe that individual family member problems, which they have silenced or not addressed, will go away in time. But they never really disappear! Rather, they lie dormant until a triggering event occurs and then awaken louder and fiercer than ever. The triggering event often is a succession in generational ownership, the retirement of the family patriarch or matriarch, or the death of a person in power.

Changing or altered circumstances resulting from life events and a normal aging process can surprise family leadership who thought everything had been agreed upon definitively for all time. They are thrown off balance when new family issues arise. It most likely was fine initially but is no longer acceptable today.

The family principals in control, either through their management or ownership positions, must recognize that the needs and desires of all family members will change over time and must be addressed and readdressed periodically without personal bias or judgment.

The crucial point is that family leadership needs to address *each* family issue at the *time of occurrence* and work doggedly to resolve the matter in a fair and equitable way to all parties affected. It does not matter whether the aggrieved party is a minority or significant shareholder. Remember, today's minority owner issues can become tomorrow's majority owner problems if not addressed.

The following chart depicts a three-phase strategy to manage family dynamics:

Conflict Avoidance & Resolution Process

I. PREVENTION

Family Council & Constitution | Outside Board | Shareholders' Agreement | Regular Communications

II. DETECTION

Individual & Family Formal & Informal Communications | Family Retreats | Stakeholder Access to CEO

III. RESOLUTION

Informal One on One Discussions | Internal Mediation | External Professional Mediation | Arbitration/Litigation

Step One—Prevention

The first step requires a "meeting of the minds" regarding the key aspects of managing the business and the family.

This is a time-consuming process that requires all stakeholders to take part in forging and agreeing to "the deal"—a comprehensive agreement on how the family will handle the diverse but typical issues that arise in family enterprises. There are both organizational and contractual issues that must be agreed upon by family ownership, along with a protocol for modifying the agreement over time as needs change.

The formal organizations and documents necessary for negotiating, finalizing, and documenting an agreed-upon deal are a family council, a family constitution, a board of directors, and a shareholders' agreement.

The family constitution and the family council are effective means for identifying and addressing *family* issues. The board of directors is charged with recognizing and addressing *business* issues, while the shareholders' agreement codifies solutions to *ownership* issues.

Examples of family issues include: Are spouses considered part of the family business? Who can participate on the family council? Do we want to have an annual extended family retreat? Who or how can family members work in the business?

Examples of business and shareholder issues include: Who gets to own the stock? How does the company terminate a family member employee? What is the policy on cash dividends or tax distributions for pass-through entities? What happens when someone dies, retires, or can no longer function in his or her job as an employee, board member, or even owner?

The process to establish an effective family council and board of directors and negotiate a family constitution and shareholders' agreement is time consuming. It requires and benefits from multiple meetings with family shareholders. It often requires individual meetings to make sure that all parties, including the less business-informed family members, understand the proposed provisions.

When developing a shareholders' agreement, the company must retain competent corporate legal counsel and, as needed, other professional advisors on taxation, estate planning, or family business management to assist. In addition, I recommend that individual family members have their own legal counsel advising them before agreeing to and signing a shareholders' agreement.

With these oversight organizations and agreements in place and agreed upon by the ownership, a family enterprise will have significantly reduced present and future family conflict.

Again, these prevention strategies should be reviewed and updated on a regular basis or as shareholder needs change. Doing so will improve a company's odds for not having a significant and disruptive family conflict. Equally important, it will help avoid a distracting and time-consuming conflict resolution process. An investment in time up front always pays good returns.

Chapter 5 provides details on creating the above organizational structures and agreements.

Step 2—Detection

After investing in time with family stakeholders and the cost of using external professionals to develop family conflict prevention strategies, management then must be alert to detect any new potential conflicts as soon as they emerge or are triggered.

The key to success is *communication, communication, communication*—at the family group level and with individual stakeholders.

While this process requires an investment in time by family leadership, it is the only sure-fire way to have a pulse on whether the family enterprise is meeting stakeholder needs, desires, and concerns at both an individual and group level. While prevention and detection may seem simple, they often are ignored. A strong and continual commitment by family leadership is necessary, beginning with involvement by family board members and the CEO.

Both formal and informal communication structures are needed to address communication. Communication can be presented at a high level to protect confidentiality where necessary. Regardless, the leaders of the business must treat family owners as investors by providing respect, access, and awareness of the successes and concerns associated with their business.

Formal communication, such as a quarterly or annual investor report, should be provided to family stakeholders over a certain age. For younger family owners or beneficiaries of trusts, a good practice is to check with their parents to have them decide what information should be provided.

The investor report could be modeled after a shareholder annual report of a public company but with less detail. One goal is simple—management never wants adult family members to hear about *their* business from others before hearing about it from the company. Sample contents to consider for an investor report include the following:

- The CEO's review and outlook for the business
- An appropriate level of financial and sales/marketing information
- An update on recent and planned projects and business strategies
- Any major organizational changes
- Any actions under consideration that impact the community and are important to shareholders

In addition to investor reports, other activities should be developed by the family council to keep the family bonded as a family. These could include providing a secure, dedicated website or secure social media site to allow family members to post family news; production of a quarterly family newsletter; and publication of a family directory with helpful contact and background information.

Many families have had great success with an annual or biannual family enterprise retreat managed by the family council. The retreat should be paid for by the business to encourage broad participation from family members throughout the country. A typical approach, if affordable, is to have family stakeholders, including future stakeholders, invited to a nice location where business, family, and fun networking activities take place.

Informal communication also helps prevent and detect potential family conflict. Individual informal meetings with the CEO or board chair are also effective in keeping family ownership informed and supportive. These individual meetings should allow time, in a relaxed and nonjudgmental setting, for reviewing such formal communications as financial statements that individual family owners may not fully understand and for checking in with individual family stakeholders.

These informal meetings also demonstrate that the business leadership *respects* each family owner as an individual. It also makes owners feel important and part of the business—something often lost in family enterprises with family ownership problems.

While addressing these formal and informal communication problems is vital for managing family dynamics, such efforts must not be a substitute for family leadership responding promptly to newly identified concerns from the ownership. As stated, individual needs change over time, and, if ignored, may become more difficult, costly, and lengthy to resolve.

Step 3—Conflict Resolution

A family member conflict not only can be difficult to resolve but it can also morph into a moving target. The biggest challenge is trying to unearth and diagnose the root cause of a conflict, which often is not the one stated.

Conflict can be triggered by an unrelated or misunderstood act. Critical listening and diagnostic skills are needed in these situations.

Many times, the true problem is only discovered and properly addressed with the help of an outside therapist or family business consultant who can help everyone involved understand the source of the conflict and possible acceptable solutions. Remember, if the root cause is not identified and resolved, then addressing the current stated conflict will only result in temporary relief. Thus, the probability of another iteration of the conflict arising in the future is high!

In multigenerational family enterprises, conflicts created from a prior generation's issues can arise even decades later. Therefore, the current generation of management may have to address "historical baggage" before permanently resolving the current conflict. Sometimes, a simple apology for the prior generation's actions is all that is needed to clean the slate for the next generation to work better together (and, of course, not repeat the offensive behavior from the prior generation).

The primary objective of a conflict resolution process is first to allow the aggrieved party to be heard. The first response of the listener should be to repeat the words of the aggrieved family member in a sincere and nonjudgmental manner.

The convener must listen for the *emotion* expressed by the unhappy family member to understand how the aggrieved party feels and then reflect that emotion back to the other person with understanding and sympathy. The technical term for this is *reflection*.

Too often, family members are not good listeners and are thinking about their next rebuttal or response instead of trying to understand the depth of grievance of the other family member. This behavior is doomed from the outset. Being a good listener is a formidable challenge. So, when a company's management selects family members to take part in conflict resolution, there must be certitude that their selected representatives possess these listening skills. Any family member that loves a good debate is not a desirable candidate to facilitate conflict resolution!

A proven conflict resolution process is one based on increasing formality, cost, and time. Organizationally, the family council should *design* the conflict resolution process, while the chair of the family council or another member not on the family council conflict resolution committee could manage the process. A key objective is to move the process along and ensure that the aggrieved party *feels properly treated and promptly heard.*

There are differing approaches for resolving family business conflict. The best of them take into consideration the participants involved and the specific family's culture.

The following four-stage conflict resolution process can serve as a starting point for your family enterprise.

Level I—One-on-One Private Meeting

A good first step is to organize a one-on-one private meeting between the aggrieved family member(s) and either the board chair or CEO. If they can resolve the matter, that is ideal. Timeliness on setting up a meeting and actually meeting is important to show the proper respect, priority, and importance of the matter.

At this juncture, the inclusion of a family therapist or business consultant often can help enormously in developing a mutually acceptable resolution. Resolving the conflict at this stage will result in the least costly, most expedient, and best result from a family relationship perspective.

Level II—Internal Mediation

If the issue is not resolvable at that juncture, the second step is to set a meeting between the aggrieved party and the family council conflict resolution committee. This committee's goal is to come up with a recommendation that both the aggrieved party and committee endorse. The family council presents the agreed-upon recommendation to the CEO or board chair for either acceptance or, if necessary, a presentation to the board of directors for approval. If the recommendation is a buy-out of the aggrieved party or a similar ownership issue, it may require shareholder approval.

Level III—External Mediation

The final step prior to litigation is external mediation managed by a professional mediator. The goal is to work out a mutually acceptable, negotiated resolution between the parties. Selecting an independent and respected mediator should be agreed upon by both parties. This step may require the use of lawyers, which will incur additional costs. And if not resolved at this juncture, litigation or arbitration typically occurs—generally resulting in a disaster for all involved.

Level IV—Arbitration or Litigation

If the above three levels fail to produce an acceptable resolution, then the final and least desirable step is arbitration or litigation. This is very expensive, stressful, and time consuming. It also can release confidential information to the public. In addition, it transfers the resolution from the family's hands to either an arbitrator or court room.

As a result, resolutions thus are based upon law rather than family or business culture, needs, or desires. This is often a significant drawback. The end result usually involves a winner and a loser, which can permanently damage family relationships and may not be in the best financial interests of the family or the family enterprise.

In conclusion, considering the costs, time, diversion of critical company and family resources, and impact on family harmony, an investment in procedures to prevent and detect family conflict is literally worth its weight in gold. It therefore should be an integral part of a family enterprise's culture and its conflict resolution strategy.

Chapter

FIVE

Family and Business Governance

*Separate governance for the family and the business is critical
for enterprise longevity, success, and family harmony.*

REMEMBER, IF YOU OWN a family enterprise, there is an 85 to 90 percent chance that it will not make it to the third generation.

Even worse, this tragic result can be accompanied by lawsuits between family members that not only destroy the business but cause financial ruin of family members and poison multigenerational family relationships. To avoid these situations, a family enterprise must develop organizational structures and governance practices as early in the company's history as possible.

Governance Challenges

In non-family-owned businesses, shareholders elect board members to represent them and oversee management and the overall affairs of the business. Business decisions are either defined in a shareholders' agreement or are delegated to the board. Family issues do not exist.

Family enterprises, however, must deal with a myriad of family personal, financial, and emotional issues on top of all the operating issues that confront any business. Addressing these family issues along with operating concerns is essential to the success and longevity of a family enterprise.

Because family stakeholders are not independent investors, the typical boundaries between shareholders, directors, managers, and family members often are disregarded or not respected. This results in overlapping and confusing organizational structures because family members have multiple and intertwined business and family roles.

In addition, family members' personal objectives often conflict with those of the operating business or family office. In my experience working with many family business clients, objectivity and independence are at times replaced with personal emotions and a desire to protect all or certain family members. Furthermore, results of actions or inactions often are not well measured, or worse, poor results are quietly excused in order to maintain good family relationships.

For example, jobs may be provided to family members based upon birthright, age, and a representation for their family branch rather than upon business need or individual capabilities. Similarly, business investment and strategic decisions can be influenced by individual family members' personal needs, which may not be in the best interests of all stakeholders.

Even processes for recruiting, motivating, and retaining high-performing nonfamily managers often are impaired because of family dynamics, frequently to the detriment of the company.

Problems become exacerbated over time, as family member needs change because of age, risk tolerance, individual holdings, marital status, income levels, lifestyle needs, and a desire to diversify holdings into other investments.

If not properly addressed, these challenges can lead to damaged family relationships, unhealthy family enterprise dynamics, and impaired business performance.

Creating a Governance Strategy

The first step to remedy these deficiencies is to implement a *governance strategy* for the family enterprise that recognizes the needs of each family stakeholder and that of the business. Family leadership must recognize that individual needs may differ from those of the business.

A good starting point is to have a series of family meetings to establish core values and guiding principles for governing the affairs of the family as they relate to the family enterprise.

The initial family meetings should begin with the drafting of a *family mission statement* and an agreement on the *family's core values and goals*, followed by a document that defines the purpose of the family enterprise and the reason for its existence.

Important questions at the first meeting might be as follows: Why do we have a family business, and why has it not been sold?

What role does the business play in the family? Is the business to be run for the family or to maximize shareholders' returns? What are individual shareholders' needs and desires from the business?

To address these issues properly and effectively, the family needs full participation from both passive and active family stakeholders in the business. (Passive stakeholders are current or future owners of the business, while active stakeholders are owners or future owners who also work in the business.)

After these and other fundamental issues have been agreed upon, the family should create *two governance organizations*—one to address family issues and the other to address business management issues. These two separate organizations are called a family council and a board of directors.

Family Governance—Family Council

The family council is responsible for representing and addressing the family issues associated with the family enterprise. The council should have representation from all family member constituents.

A family council is composed of family members and current and possibly future owners who will establish rules and oversight regarding family issues associated with the family enterprise. It provides direction to the board of directors on family expectations and the family's culture, including how the company treats its community, employees, customers, and suppliers.

It can also specify general business direction, acceptable risks, expected returns, cash distributions, and similar business-related issues. Another common responsibility is regular communication with the extended family via newsletters, quarterly update meetings, and an annual retreat that includes both a business review and fun family networking activities.

The first steps in creating a family council are structural and should be developed with input at family meetings from active and passive family enterprise stakeholders. Here are some issues to consider:

- How many members will serve on the family council?
- How will members be elected or appointed?
- Are there term limits or other restrictions (e.g., only so many members from a specific branch of the family)?
- Are there minimum requirements for membership (e.g., age, education, business experience, family representation, current shareholder, current executive of company)?
- What reporting and communications will be provided to the extended family and the board of directors and at what frequency?
- What guidelines will control the determination of family council compensation and leadership?
- What frequency of family meetings is ideal, and who will be invited to these meetings?

Family council meetings should be professionally run, like a board of directors, with regular formal meetings. They should take place at least annually and often quarterly, depending upon circumstances, and have strict attendance requirements. Relevant reports and other essential materials should be sent in advance to all members at least ten days prior to a meeting. In addition, member participation and performance should be evaluated annually to maintain a high-functioning family council.

Key agenda items to consider for family council meetings include the following:

- Developing an annual business plan detailing expected accomplishments, funding requirements, responsibility assignments, and completion dates, with milestones that allow performance to be measured.

- Establishing and communicating shareholder financial goals to the board as they relate to risk, long-term investment returns, cash distributions, wealth management, and diversification objectives.

- Planning an annual family business retreat that includes considerations for the event, such as budget, location, agenda, attendee expense reimbursement policy, presentation materials, breakout sessions, education plans, outside speakers, and family play time or networking.

- Developing written guidelines for hiring, professional development and educational planning, succession planning, termination procedures for employed family members, and membership on the board or family council.

- Handling problems within the family and facilitating conflict resolution.

- Providing family council feedback to the CEO or board members.

Family Governance—Family Constitution

A key initial task for the family council is to develop a *family constitution*. This document outlines the rules, responsibilities, and rights of family members. It addresses their involvement with the business and participation in various family and business organizations discussed therein. It should be customized to meet a family's needs and culture and can be detail oriented or general.

A typical constitution table of contents could include the following:

1. Family history
2. Family vision statement
3. Family values statement
4. Code of conduct for family members and business associates
5. Overview of the business
6. Owners of the business
7. Responsibilities and authority level definitions for the different roles that family members assume in the business (e.g., owner, director, employee, family member)
8. Guidelines, regulations, and responsibilities for family and business governance
9. Family employment guidelines for hiring, continued employment, retirement, and termination
10. Initiatives that benefit both family members and the company, such as internships and educational support
11. Social media and confidentiality guidelines
12. Conflict resolution processes
13. Other family policies

Particularly in periods of ownership transition, the family council should provide input to update (or initially develop) a shareholders' agreement. This agreement, signed by all owners, contractually binds the ownership to decisions made on predetermined business and ownership matters. The ownership, board of directors, and family council must follow its directives.

Ownership Governance—Shareholders' Agreement

A shareholders' agreement outlines the rules by which the owners of the business will function together. The agreement addresses issues such as:

- Who can own equity?
- What options and restrictions should be established for selling or transferring ownership interests? What rules should govern company and family members' ownership purchase rights of first refusal?
- What is the desirable size and meeting frequency for the board of directors, and what criteria should govern the electing of its members (e.g., number of family members, number of outside independent directors, term limits)?
- What are the requirements for approving major transactions, such as a sale of assets, a major financing, capital calls, large capital expenditures, etc.?
- What valuation methodology for stock/ownership interests should be used?
- What rights will minority shareholders have on specific decisions or when supermajority ownership votes are required?
- What is the policy for cash distributions, including a policy of providing funds to the owners for pass-through business income tax liabilities?

- What is the policy for hiring or terminating family member employment?

A shareholders' agreement (also known as an owners' operating agreement, LLC operating agreement, or partnership agreement, depending on the form of organization) should be tailored to your family's needs and culture. It can be as broad or detailed as desired.

It is always better to negotiate this agreement before actual issues arise from a situation or shareholder request. Parties will be more neutral in their positions when their personal stakes in the outcome are not the immediate focus of the discussion.

While there are standard corporate laws to guide running a business, a shareholders' agreement will override standard corporate law. Therefore, all owners need to sign the agreement. I always recommend that each family member be represented by legal counsel prior to signing this agreement.

The following is a list of topics I typically discuss when assisting clients and their attorneys with developing a shareholders' agreement (see the detailed checklist in Appendix B):

1. Types of ownership interests and rights (e.g., voting, nonvoting, restricted)
2. Board representation, governance, and oversight
3. Dividend distribution policies
4. Debt level authorization procedure
5. Capital expenditure and investment approval
6. Capital calls and dilution guidelines
7. Sale of company ("drag-along" or "come-along/tag-along" rights)

8. Stock put option to provide liquidity for minority shareholders

9. Rights of first refusals and preemptive rights

10. Transfer restrictions

11. Triggering events for buy-sell provisions (e.g., employment termination, retirement, disability, death)

12. Valuation of shares and ownership interests

13. Ownership redemption notes, terms and conditions

14. Funding strategies for buy-sell transactions

15. Default and remedies

Business Governance—Board of Directors and Board Committees

The second essential organizational structure, the board of directors, focuses on the business and represents *all* shareholders. Members are elected by the shareholders or appointed, based upon the terms outlined in a shareholders' agreement.

Best practice is to include a minimum of two to three outside and independent (nonfamily) directors on the board to maintain an objective balance of oversight and management accountability on behalf of the shareholders.

The outside or independent directors can be fiduciary directors, with voting rights and the assumption of associated director liability, or advisory (nonvoting) directors who therefore have significantly reduced director liability.

When using advisory directors, be certain they have the same rights and compensation of fiduciary directors (except for voting privileges). In family businesses, voting is not an important factor. The major benefit of independent board members is their expertise and engagement in discussions that *influence* decision-making.

The role of family and outside directors is to represent all shareholders and not individual family members or even family branches. Unfortunately, when family feuds creep into the family business, family member directors often revert to their family branches and no longer focus on what is best for the overall shareholder group.

Family business boards are not informal family meetings. They need to be professionally run. Nonfamily directors help insure a level of professionalism, mutual respect, objectivity, and formality for family business board meetings.

I often recommend creating up to three standing board of director committees: executive committee, compensation committee, and audit committee, depending on the size, complexity, and family culture of the business.

Executive Committee

The executive committee is helpful when the company has a large board of directors and regular board decisions need to be made in between board meetings. The executive committee can be empowered by the board to make certain decisions on behalf of the full board in lieu of a board meeting. The other alternative is to have interim board telephone or videoconference calls where decisions can be made. For routine resolutions not requiring board discussion, a *unanimous consent resolution without a board meeting* document, if signed by all fiduciary directors, is another way for board approvals.

Compensation Committee

The compensation committee is particularly beneficial when there are multiple family members employed in management. Family compensation administered by siblings or parents can be problematic and, at times, can create major problems among the family ownership.

The initial challenge is to objectively determine *equitable* compensation among family member employees. An additional challenge is to determine the rewards for ownership (i.e., distributions) and how they relate to the rewards for employment (i.e., compensation). These two separate but at times related reward structures are very difficult to manage solely by family leadership. If not done carefully, the result can be family rifts in and outside of the family enterprise.

Creating a formal compensation committee composed of non-family directors or advisors provides a large degree of comfort to family members that compensation practices and owner distributions are fair and appropriate.

Having a family business engage an independent consulting firm to complete a market-based compensation benchmarking study for each management position is a best practice. Their compensation report would provide real-world comparable data on base pay, incentives, and total compensation for 25th, 50th, and 75th percentiles for similar businesses (e.g., industry, size, geographic location).

Sharing the report with the family helps reach a consensus on what is fair. After reviewing the study's assumptions, data inputs, and conclusions, the family might make adjustments to the study's recommendations to reflect issues raised or uncovered during these meetings to best fit with the family's culture and desires.

The important point is that final decisions are made on the

basis of a solid factual foundation that has been shared with all impacted stakeholders.

At the completion of the study and discussion process, compensation and owner distribution and dividend practices are agreed upon and are hopefully acceptable to the family, thus fulfilling the goal of the process.

Audit (or Finance) Committee

The audit committee is helpful when the family, external financial institutions, or investors want to be certain that the business results and financial condition are independently reviewed and are well controlled from a financial perspective. Best practice is to have the auditing firm report directly to the audit committee, not the management team. A key deliverable, in addition to audited financial statements, should be an internal control report with recommendations for improvements in accounting, reporting, and control procedures.

Board of Director Benefits

Many benefits result when outside independent directors join a family business board. Ideally, these directors contribute broad skills and business experience that the family business management team and other directors do not possess. Typical benefits include:

1. Holding the management team accountable for plans, strategies, financial results, risk management, and organizational development;

2. Raising sensitive issues that otherwise might be "swept under the rug," such as inadequate planning or lack of succession plans;

—These first two points are difficult to accomplish when only family members sit on a board.

3. Providing "door openings" for new business contacts, management talent, and access to the external business community, along with other beneficial networking opportunities;

4. Providing an objective and neutral balance between family issues and business issues;

5. Enhancing the credibility of the business by providing independent governance and oversight for external stakeholders, such as banks, investors, customers, suppliers, management team, and passive family member owners; and

6. Providing opportunities for offline, one-on-one confidential consultations outside of the board room with the CEO or other senior executives.

I have found that current or prior CEOs who have successfully implemented business plans similar to those of the family business make excellent board members. While many directors are skilled at evaluating business strategies and plans, CEOs have the unique experience to understand the human and financial resources that are necessary to *implement* strategies and plans successfully.

Because needs change along with plans, specified board term limits are helpful to facilitate electing new directors who are better equipped to meet evolving business challenges. Staggered terms also should be considered to maintain legacy knowledge.

Creating Your Board of Directors

The first steps are to determine the size of the board, the number of family directors and outside independent directors, and the meeting frequency.

The next step is to define the necessary skill and experience requirements desired in a board member through a process of focused objectivity. This requires evaluating the skills of the current management and board and then identifying the gaps or additional skills needed to implement the specified business strategies.

The following grid is one I have used frequently for clients, customized for the specific experience or skill requirements of a particular family enterprise. The recommended approach is to add columns to the grid for senior executives and existing directors and complete the grid for each person.

Finally, the family should review, determine, and specify the skills needed to complement the existing team. Needs change over time, so the grid should be updated when replacing termed-out directors. This step complements the guideline by which directors and advisors are engaged for three-year terms and subject to renewal only if their skills are still essential to the company or for other compelling reasons.

An equally important step is to assess director candidates on his or her qualitative skills—those that help assure the compatibility of a potential director with the company and the family. These skills can be described as follows:

Board Member Selection Assessment Matrix
Experience/Skills/Knowledge Rating

Board	Private Company Board Experience
	Family Business Board Experience
	Financial/Audit Committee Experience
	Compensation Committee Experience
Leadership	CEO Experience in a Mid-Size Growth Company
	Experience in Developing a Management Team
	Fit with Company Culture & People
Industry	Specific Industry Experience & Knowledge
	Important Industry Contacts
	Industry "Name" Recognition
Family Business	Family Business Management & Leadership
	Family & Business Governance
	Family Dynamics & Shareholder Relations
	Family Succession Planning
	Shareholder Issues & Estate Planning
Strategy	Strategic Planning
	Business Planning
	Strategy Implementation
Marketing, Sales & PR	Sales Management
	New Product/Services Development
	Distribution Channel Development
	Internet Commerce
	Viral Marketing/Social Media Marketing
	International Marketing and Sales Development
	Public, Government & Industry Relations
Operations	Job Shop or Repetitive Manufacturing
	Manufacturing Mgmt. Systems/Performance
	Outsourcing/Vendor-Contractor Management
	Logistic & Distribution Management
	International Sourcing/Manufacturing
Finance	Financial Management, Planning & Analysis
	Accounting, Auditing & Internal Controls
	Cash Management/Forecasting
	Cost and Profitability Accounting
	Capital Raising & Deal Structure
IT/Technology	Information Systems Planning & Implementation
	Technology to Enhance Customer/Vendor Experience
	Data Security & Loss Prevention

Personal Traits

- High ethical standards, professional demeanor, and relevant experiences
- Significant track record of success
- Good interpersonal skills
- Care and concern for the family and the business
- Ability and willingness to be candid, honest, and forthright in a thoughtful, team-oriented manner
- Adequate time availability and firm commitment to attend all meetings and conference calls

Independence

- No other business relationship with the family company that could create a conflict of interest (e.g., lawyers, accountants, suppliers, customers)
- A commitment to policies that advance the overall value of the company for *all* shareholders, as opposed to those that benefit only specific family member ownership or employment interests

Track Record

- Significant successful track record in business, preferably as a CEO or president
- Solid educational and professional background with some relevance to the family business

- Experience in multiple functional areas and industries that allow for a broad perspective
- Experience serving on other business and/or non-profit boards

Diversity

- Individuals who bring a breadth of diversity of experience and perspective to the boardroom

Compatibility

- Individuals with whom family members generally feel comfortable and welcome being associated with in a business environment
- Individuals who are respected and trusted so that their advice is properly received and valued

Best Operating Practices for Boards

Based upon experience as an advisor to boards and having personally served on fifteen business boards, I suggest considering the following operating practices for a family enterprise board.

1. Choose someone other than the CEO as board chair, even a passive shareholder, so that issues of concern to shareholders not actively involved with the business are addressed.

2. Establish a standard baseline agenda for meetings so that certain key metrics, initiatives, and business issues are always addressed.

3. Code agenda items as *discussion*, *informational only*, or *decision required* to better inform directors and keep meetings focused and efficient. Minimize presentation time for informational materials that are sent out in advance (typically one to two weeks prior to a meeting).

4. Establish a board meeting calendar for an entire year at least three months prior to the beginning of the year.

5. Invite senior executives to sit in for part of each meeting or ask them to make a board presentation to expose the senior management team's capabilities to the board.

6. Institute an annual off-site strategy retreat with the board and key executives.

7. Develop written annual business and financial plans that require board approval; create a strong planning and review process within the company.

8. Establish an independent, director-based compensation committee to address senior executive compensation and, if audited, an audit committee to obtain feedback directly from the auditors.

9. Have the board chair conduct an annual or biannual performance review of each board member; evaluation criteria should include board member meeting attendance, preparedness, participation (constructive), and interpersonal skills.

10. Develop succession and contingency plans to manage specific risks (e.g., loss of CEO, critical customer or supplier, or financing).

11. Establish minimum meeting attendance, age or term limits, independence, and conflict of interest rules for all board members.

12. Offer competitive board compensation (excluding company executives) for meetings, phone calls, business-related travel, and committee participation.

13. Facilitate board member visits to company facilities and operations.

Establishing an effective family council, board of directors, family constitution, and shareholders' agreement will help ensure that the needs and interests of both the enterprise and the family will be addressed and met—separately, effectively, and compatibly.

These governance organizations will help support and produce the ongoing success of a multigenerational family enterprise with all of its family members.

Chapter

SIX

Toxic Family Enterprise Boards

It takes only one toxic director to destroy your board. Learn from five case studies how to recognize the risk and prevent it from disabling your board.

FAMILY BUSINESSES AND FAMILY offices require an effective board of directors for fiduciary and governance oversight like other public and privately held businesses. In addition, family business boards are uniquely important, as they augment the skills and experience of the smaller-sized management teams associated with many family enterprises.

Boards provide independence, objectivity, relevant external business experiences, and broad shareholder representation. Many family enterprises attribute their success to an effective and supportive board of directors or board of advisors (nonfiduciary board).

I have witnessed both effective and ineffective boards, the latter creating frustration and sometimes fatal problems for company management and fellow board members.

Any board's performance depends upon group dynamics. This becomes challenging for family businesses if one director becomes toxic by virtue of behavior that undermines management or the board. As will be shown, *every* director's ability to work successfully within a group is critical to the performance of the entire board.

That is not to say that a director must be compliant or go along with so-called "group think." Quite the contrary, every director should feel comfortable to voice a strong and well-reasoned minority position or concern. Directors should be critical thinkers, independent and respectful, but never confrontational, abusive, or petty.

Since positive group dynamics are essential to board effectiveness, prospective directors should be evaluated for their interpersonal and communication skills in addition to their technical and business expertise. Both criteria should be carefully considered when electing either family members or outside independent directors or advisors to a board.

Having served on two public company and thirteen privately owned (mainly family business) boards and a dozen nonprofit boards over the years, I have observed numerous examples where one director significantly derailed the effectiveness of the entire board! In certain instances, as discussed in the case studies below, a single director caused so much disruption that key board fiduciary duties and directives became sidelined by irrelevant "pet-peeve" issues and personal biases, much to the detriment of the enterprise's operating performance.

Case Study 1—The "Founder Knows Best" Director

This fiduciary board was established by the founder and 95 percent owner of a first-generation financial services family business. The company, despite being significantly undercapitalized, had achieved a successful thirty-year track record, due to the tenacity and skills of its founder/CEO.

As business conditions tightened and profits declined during the Great Recession of 2008, the board directed the CEO and CFO to raise equity capital to support the growing asset base of the firm. The founder/CEO, however, wanted to raise subordinated debt. He was more concerned about dilution than bringing in equity capital. The board was concerned about *survival*.

To placate the board, the CEO proceeded in an effort to raise equity capital but adamantly insisted upon unrealistic valuations for the stock. Not surprisingly, the CEO failed in all instances to close an equity transaction.

In the end, equity was not raised because the CEO ignored the advice of his outside board. The company was forced to fold due to lack of capital after an unanticipated turn for the worse in the business. This example of the "founder knows best" director who did not listen to his independent board resulted in the founder losing his company and the equity he had built over his thirty years of success.

If your family business has an independent, experienced, and capable board, then listen to them. If you don't have a strong independent board, then create one (see chapter 5).

Case Study 2—The "Family Branch Protector" Director

This board represented the shareholders of a third- and fourth-generation family-owned chemical business. The board was composed of six family members, one of whom was president and another was vice president. There were *no* independent nonfamily directors, a fatal flaw known by all of us involved in family business consulting.

The six directors came from four family branches. The primary goal of all was to grow the family business for the next generation and maintain family harmony and relationships. However, with a lack of outside and independent directors, it became very difficult for the family board to hold the family management team accountable.

While intentions were initially good, under this lack of independent board oversight and management accountability, results declined over a period of years. During this decline, the board chair's perspective migrated from one that represented all shareholders to one biased toward protecting the disappointing performance of his brother, the president. As this bias intensified, the other board members became disgruntled and moved toward representing *their* family branch's interests, at times to the impairment of the family business.

Family dynamics eroded, and the environment became political and divisive. Unfortunately, the business continued to decline, contributing to increasingly poor relationships among the extended family. In the end, the family business suffered from weak performance, dissatisfied shareholders, unhappy executives (including one who left the business), and strained family relationships.

Boards need to represent all shareholders, not family branches, and need to include outside and independent board members to provide additional professionalism, objectivity, and management accountability.

Case Study 3—The Conflicted Director

This board represented the shareholders of a third-generation family manufacturing business. The board was composed of several family members, most of whom worked for the company, and three outside and independent nonfamily directors. Initially, the board was very high functioning and professionally run.

The three outside directors helped create the formality and structure needed for professional board meetings. The board held annual strategy retreats with senior executives and focused on the right issues. The business was growing by double digits in both its top and bottom lines. The management team continued expanding, adding nonfamily executives who helped drive further growth.

A major problem arose, however, when one of the outside independent directors lost his job (unrelated to the family company on whose board he served) and attempted to start up new personal business ventures not relevant to the family company. This director ("conflicted director") wanted the family business to be the major investor in his various new ventures. This put the CEO in the awkward position of evaluating business deals for the family business that were proposed by one of his independent directors.

In the end, the CEO, with other board members' concurrence, rejected all the investments in the conflicted director's proposed businesses. The CEO was directed by the board to request of this director that he not present any more proposals to the board for investment. This created tension and anger with the director, who then used his position on the board and relationships with various other family members to undermine the CEO. It quickly became personal.

While business results continued to exceed expectations, turmoil and unrest in the boardroom eventually began affecting senior executives. The other two outside directors refused to intervene to address either the internal family issues or the conflicted director's destructive role in the boardroom.

The problematic family and board member dynamics that had been triggered by one disgruntled and conflicted director led this highly successful third-generation family business to be sold as a means to pacify various family stakeholders.

Be certain to have term limits and a written conflict of interest policy among other policies to which board members must agree prior to their appointment to the board. If such a conflict occurs within the term of a board member, the chair, in most instances, should facilitate removing the member from the board.

Case Study 4—The "Policeman/Witch-Hunt" Director

This board represented the owners of a real estate company where an outside property management firm was engaged. The mission of the board was typical: oversee management's effectiveness and approve basic business policies, operating and capital expenditure budgets, property improvement plans, and risk assessments. The directors were functioning effectively and working well with management.

However, after two years, one board member was replaced with a new director. The new director had considerable real estate development and management experience and, on paper, appeared to be a great addition to the board. He was hardworking, energetic, and quite smart about the business. He became a strong and active director who initially won the appreciation of his fellow directors and management.

However, after a year, this director began to show several toxic traits that changed the entire dynamics of the board and its relationship with the management team.

He became excessively skeptical and distrusting of management and changed from a supportive director to one primarily focused on "catching" management doing something unacceptable in his eyes. In this "policeman" role, the director became adversarial and disruptive both in and out of board meetings. He took it upon himself to take initiatives directly with management and with outside business suppliers that were not discussed or approved by the board.

He constantly challenged management and regularly confused his role as a director with that of management. He lost objectivity and made serious accusations that could not be substantiated. He became a "loose cannon" and created havoc throughout the company. Relationships deteriorated significantly in his interactions with his fellow directors and management.

As a result, the board became dysfunctional. One of the key directors resigned, and issues that required board attention were circumvented due to the crises this lone director was creating. Owners became dissatisfied as they heard directly from this rogue director about various issues that either turned out not to be true or not of any significance.

The basic governance process of the board was hijacked by this director's actions. In the end, this director was forced off the board. He wrote an apologetic letter to the board, the owners, and the management company and resigned in disgrace. Unfortunately for the owners, two years were lost in addressing key issues and a significant amount of funds were expended on legal fees and other nonproductive activities created by this director.

Have an empowered board chair keep directors from functioning as management. Directors have no power individually other than voting for or against board actions and participating in boardroom discussions.

Case Study 5—The Lackadaisical Directors

This four-member board oversaw a start-up technology company. After losing one director for personal reasons, the board dropped to three directors: two outsiders and the founder/CEO. For years, the board was unofficially controlled by the CEO/founder due to a hands-off board.

As one might expect, the board under this situation represented the CEO's interest, which at times conflicted with the shareholders' interests. The board finally added another director and was again composed of three outsiders and the founder/CEO. Unfortunately, the outside directors still did not challenge the strong-willed CEO. While he was a great promoter, he was a poor businessman who never delivered on his projected results.

The company continued to lose money and impair its capital base. The three outside directors became more complacent over time. They were afraid to challenge the technically proficient CEO, in part because the company did not have backup resources to replace him. The board became a rubber stamp and hostage to the CEO's thinking. As a result, the CEO became even more nonresponsive to the board.

Eventually, the company went into Chapter 7 bankruptcy when its external financings were pulled. The ultimate irony is that the board learned about the bankruptcy after the fact and two hours prior to the CEO emailing the shareholders that the business had been shut down.

The investors lost their entire investment, several customers lost prepaid service contracts, and the CEO lost most of his personal assets, along with his reputation.

This company ran without an *effective* independent board and ended up as a disaster for all involved.

Boards have a fiduciary responsibility and legal liability to the shareholders. Family businesses must be certain that their board is overseeing the business responsibly and representing the shareholders' interests, not those of management or a subset of special interest shareholders.

Toxic Director Characteristics

Toxic directors can come from any part of the board—the CEO, founders or owners, and inside or external board members. It takes only one toxic director to impact the effectiveness of a board.

Each case study above demonstrates the failure of a board to function effectively. None of the reasons for poor board performance were due to incompetence of the board members but rather from the subtle issues of how directors functioned in a group. Careful evaluation of these qualitative issues must be included in any assessment of prospective new board members for a family enterprise.

Chapter

SEVEN

Succession Planning

Overcome the #1 problem with family enterprises:
inadequate succession planning.

SUCCESSION PLANNING IS ONE of the most discussed issues among family enterprise owners, yet one of the least addressed effectively. In fact, only 23 percent of US family businesses even have a written succession plan, according to PwC's most recent US Family Business Survey.

Worse yet, most succession plans that are developed fail to deal with a multitude of the quantitative and qualitative issues necessary for the proper transition of a family enterprise to the next generation.

Succession planning—or a less threatening name, continuity planning—can be a difficult subject for the current generation to face. Such discussions often trigger a range of deep emotions, among them fear, conscious acknowledgement of personal aging and death, personal identity defined by involvement in the business, and a desire to avoid family conflict. These and other personal factors contribute to the company leadership's *lack of will* to address succession planning on a timely basis, despite prodding by the next generation.

I understand these emotions; however, a transition *will* take place, whether it is planned or unplanned. However, the results of unplanned transitions generally are littered with problems that often prove devastating to the company's finances and family relationships.

Transitions occur due to death, disability, health challenges, family disputes, and other life events. Being armed with a well-thought-out succession plan, however, offers an essential advantage to those families seriously concerned about continuing family enterprise ownership and success into the next generation.

Problems with Succession Plans

Too many succession plans only identify the next CEO and update the family's estate plans. Critical and existential issues on ownership, governance, organizational development, financial and retirement planning, and business strategy often are not addressed. These issues impact the health and very survival of the business and should be considered and addressed *years before* a generational transition is forced upon the company.

The lack or inadequacy of a comprehensive succession plan also creates problems for the *existing business* prior to a transition. For example, key managers and employees need to believe that the company will survive beyond the aging current generation's ownership and leadership. Their careers, livelihood, and family security depend on it. Customers, both current and prospective, want to be comfortable with the knowledge that the business will survive and continue to support their needs in the future. Similarly, suppliers will be concerned about maintaining long-lasting supply relationships.

Unfortunately, when companies are in flux or without clear direction on succession, they suffer negative impacts to both their existing business and their business after the inevitable transition. Specific problems include recruiting and retention of management, ability to capture new customers, limitations in obtaining bank financing, poor decision-making processes due to excessive risk avoidance, and a lack of vital long-term strategic planning.

A well-designed succession plan must address the broad needs and concerns of the current generation, the next generation, employees, and all other related stakeholders—any suppliers, customers, competitors, banks, and others affected by the future success or decline of the company.

A Personal Succession Planning Case Study

I grew up in a very entrepreneurial and successful family business run by a talented and savvy Gen 2 entrepreneurial leader, George Isaac Jr. (my father). He was a hard worker, did not delegate authority or responsibility, and made most decisions for the management team. During his tenure, he started numerous businesses, including industrial scrap metals processing and recycling, car and truck tire recapping, a Goodyear tire dealership, a Chrysler-Plymouth auto dealership, car leasing, and real estate development.

The other family members working in the business were my two uncles, two aunts, and two cousins. As a result, the senior management team was 100 percent family, except for two outside managers.

When I completed my MBA at the University of Michigan, the family offered me a job in the business. At that time, it was focused on two divisions: industrial scrap metals processing and recycling, and real estate development and management. Having both grown up in a family business and worked there for several summers in my school years, I had concerns about joining the business without having outside work experience. I decided to accept an offer as a management consultant in Chicago at Deloitte Consulting.

Eight years later, my father wanted to step back and partially retire. I was offered the position of president, in part because Gen 2's autocratic management style prevented sufficient development of any internal staff. Thus, my father was unwilling to consider any of them worthy of assuming the top job.

At that time, I chose to continue my career at Deloitte. I suggested and supported the hiring of a nonfamily executive to be president. The company retained a search firm and recruited a new president/COO, who, unfortunately, did not work out well.

Within one year, my cousins asked me to become the CEO of our family's business and thus solve the problem of a poorly functioning new president/COO. I was then a partner at Deloitte Consulting. Nonetheless, I accepted the offer because I wanted to help carry on the family business for another generation, which was a strong goal of both the Gen 2 and Gen 3 family members.

Prior to resigning from my partnership in a top-tier international consulting firm, I wanted to be certain that the transition from Gen 2 to Gen 3 would be successful. I knew there would be differing needs and interests among the family members, because the company did not employ several Gen 3 shareholders.

In addition, each family member saw the business as his or her dad's business. This resulted in a range of expectations that needed to be reconciled. I also had concerns about Gen 2 "hanging on" too long. The business was the center of their lives, and *retirement* was not a word found in our family's vocabulary—and still isn't, witness my ninety-nine-year-old Aunt Marion who still comes into the office every day!

Relying on the help of outside advisors and my years of management consulting experience, I developed a succession planning road map to transition our family business to my generation, with me as CEO. This was a predecessor to the nine-step succession planning road map presented later in this chapter. The plan worked extremely well and became a critical instrument in producing the family business success that followed.

The first step in our succession plan was to obtain agreement among the shareholders on the direction and ownership goals of my generation. Based on those discussions, we restructured the ownership group. Specifically, we bought out the uninvolved Gen 3 family owners to provide them liquidity and safety versus ownership and risk. In essence, they received their financial inheritance from the wealth created by the prior generation, their parents, as part of the transition. The remaining five shareholders, my one brother and three cousins (from three family branches), each accepted a realignment of existing ownership interests. We now would be equal 20 percent shareholders.

We also negotiated a detailed shareholders' agreement that specified how we were going to function as owners after the transition to Gen 3 (i.e., "the deal"). We addressed ownership, family member employment, governance, voting rights, authority levels, distributions, capital funding guidelines, and ownership transfer rights and restrictions.

In addition, we created our family's first high-functioning professional board of directors composed of my Gen 2 father, the five Gen 3 shareholders, and three outside and independent fiduciary directors. I, as CEO, reported to the board, not my father. I had an employment contract outlining my compensation, annual bonus calculation (based upon metrics), duties, and authority levels.

We set shareholder goals and developed a strategic plan for achieving those goals. I made sure all of this planning was agreed upon prior to my signing an employment agreement and joining the business as CEO.

The results of our comprehensive succession planning were aligned shareholder goals, agreed-upon business strategies, and an empowered and expanded management team; in short, a much different way of running the business than that of the prior generation.

Although we frustrated Gen 2 family members at times due to the different management style and culture, our results were impressive. The business grew six fold over eight years, with shareholder value increasing significantly.

I have updated the road map that I first used for my family business transition, basing the changes on my several years of experience as CEO and my subsequent family business consulting work. It captures the complexity and breadth of issues that need to be addressed in a family enterprise succession plan.

When followed diligently, the road map produces a generational succession that survives the test of time and meets both the business and personal needs of the family owners.

Nine-Step Succession Planning Road Map

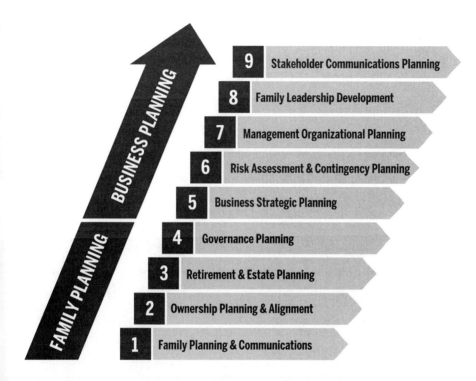

9 Stakeholder Communications Planning

8 Family Leadership Development

7 Management Organizational Planning

6 Risk Assessment & Contingency Planning

5 Business Strategic Planning

4 Governance Planning

3 Retirement & Estate Planning

2 Ownership Planning & Alignment

1 Family Planning & Communications

BUSINESS PLANNING

FAMILY PLANNING

1. Family Planning and Communications

The objective of the first step of the road map is to communicate to the family any decisions that have been reached or are being *contemplated. It is important to explain the rationale behind them so there is no misinterpretation or misunderstanding of intentions. This step also provides an opportunity to tailor the plans to meet individual family member needs and concerns.*

Most family members understand that transitioning a family enterprise to the next generation triggers many issues for both the current and next generation. Certain issues are emotional by definition—who is "picked" to be the CEO, who "gets" to own stock, who is "on the board" (in control of the enterprise), and the equitability of the financial arrangements. These are decisions that impact family members' roles, sense of purpose, and even sense of self-worth.

When money and relatives are intermingled, family dynamics issues can become heated and troublesome.

Assumptions will be made, silently or vocally, based on various family members' expectations, intentions, and motivations. Some members can be extra sensitive to certain issues because of events that occurred well in the past, frequently as far back as their childhood.

Unfortunately, succession decisions are often interpreted by the next generation as a measure of how well they are regarded, or even loved, by their family members compared to others in the family. This results in possible misinterpretations of the prior generation's decisions, which often erode next-generation relationships. These factors can negatively impact the family and the future performance of the enterprise.

The best strategies call for clear communications, full transparency, and full involvement by all who are affected. While this process is not a voting exercise, it is an important step in assuring that all family members understand *why decisions were made* and *what they do (and do not) mean* for each of them.

Achieving consensus on succession plans among all family stakeholders is a best practice and should be a key goal in any succession plan.

A good starting point is to conduct family meetings to discuss the big picture of your family and the family enterprise—in other words, the roles played and involvement and interests of all generations of stakeholders. Some recommended discussion items include the following. Family members should also be offered the opportunity to suggest additional topics.

- What are our family's core values? ("What does it mean to be a Jones?")
- What are the prior generation's wishes for the current generation and for the future of the family?
- Why do we have a family enterprise?
- Why do we want to pass it on to the next generation?
- What are our family's philosophies on money?
- What are our family's thoughts on philanthropy?
- Where do we want to be in ten years as a family and as a family enterprise?

The next generation should discuss all of the major decisions affecting ownership and management in order to find common ground and to create full support among the owners. Discussion on *how* decisions should be made and *why* resolved decisions are "fair" are equally important to discuss.

The family members should recognize that there are no right or wrong answers. Conditions and needs often vary by individual. For example, one stakeholder might want financial security and a predictable cash flow while another may prefer higher business risk in return for potentially longer-term wealth creation.

Here is a real-world example:

A recent family member client of mine had 95 percent of his net worth in a Gen 3 family real estate business. With minimal income from other sources, this client relied upon family business distributions for ongoing financial support. His minority interest in the family business provided him no authority or even a board seat. He was dissatisfied with how the business was being managed, and the cash distributions were inadequate to meet his financial requirements.

The family members in charge of the business were large shareholders, financially well off, and highly conservative in their business decisions. They wanted to keep distributions low and retain earnings for additional long-term real estate projects. There was a serious misalignment of ownership goals among the family.

It was obvious to me that the family member with minimal income would be better served financially by ending his participation in the family business. He *needed to have* a diversified investment portfolio that generated cash flow to meet his family's financial obligations. Had the prior generation considered his individual situation, a family financial plan could have been developed to satisfy this individual and create a more aligned family shareholder group for those family owners remaining in the business.

The lesson is that honest communications and transparency about individual and group needs enable most families to tailor their plans to meet the financial objectives of the next generation while also advancing the best interests of the family enterprise.

Family planning has a nonfinancial component as well. Family members not involved in the operations of the family business typically want to feel "part of" the family enterprise. Many family members see the family business as their "dad's (or mom's) business" and want some level of inclusion. Creating additional entities beyond the family business is an effective way to allow more family members to be engaged in the family enterprise.

Examples of possible entities include a family foundation, passive investment vehicles that manage family funds, and special private equity investments that align with the skills and interests of certain family members.

This approach provides the opportunity for various family members to opt in or opt out of various entities based upon their interests, skills, and financial needs. The following is a simple family enterprise illustration that supports inclusion and engagement from three generations of a family—even with room for in-laws!

Family Enterprise "End Game"

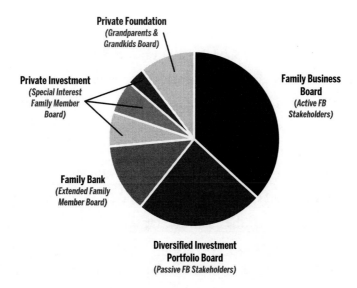

This first step of planning and communications lays the foundation for the rest of the succession planning process. Once family issues are reconciled between the current and next-generation family members, then the family is able to address the next step, ownership planning and alignment.

2. Ownership Planning and Alignment

The objective of this section is to create an aligned ownership group with compatible goals and approaches for running the family enterprise after a transition. This requires a periodic revisiting of ownership goals, as they will change over time.

Meeting owners' goals seems obvious. While well intentioned, *assumptions* are regularly made by the current generation about the next generation's goals, concerns, and tolerance for risk. These assumptions, however, often are faulty and lead to poor planning decisions.

Determining next-generation family member goals is complicated. Members of the next generation often are not candid with their parents to avoid appearing greedy or unappreciative. Or parents may feel that their children are "lucky" to inherit the business and should be satisfied and appreciative for whatever goes their way and on whatever terms the parents decide.

Unfortunately, if there is not a full and honest understanding of each individual's true feelings and needs, a succession plan will not survive once the prior generation is no longer engaged or involved in the family enterprise. I have seen this occur many times, resulting in varying degrees of problematic family dynamics and strains on the business.

When the current owners of the family enterprise desire to retain the business for the future, the next generation must reach agreement *independently* on whether they desire to retain ownership in the business and, if so, for how long. When certain owners are focused on receiving cash, either from a business sale or recurring annual distributions, and other owners want to retain capital for growth, family problems will occur.

There are many factors that should be considered to reach agreement:

- From a business perspective, is the business well positioned for future growth and success?

- From the current generation's perspective, do they have adequate financial resources to retire and still meet their financial needs?

- From the next generation's perspective, do they want to continue to own the business *and* own it with their fellow family members?

At times, there is an option to spin off the existing business into multiple asset classes to meet individual needs. For example, an operating company could distribute its physical facilities (e.g., plant and warehousing) into a separate real estate company.

This would allow certain family members to own a real estate business that leases its facilities to the operating business. These family members would receive predictable cash distributions that are supported by real estate assets. Other family members would own the operating business, which is a riskier asset but one with greater potential for upside wealth creation.

For families with family offices or significant family investments, creating different investment entities based upon certain characteristics—such as asset class, risk, liquidity, yield, and expected returns—allow individual family members to opt in or opt out of an investment based on their individual needs. This creates an all-embracing structure that meets both individual and overall family needs.

If the decision is to continue the family enterprise for another generation, then the next step is to agree how the next generation of family owners will operate together as an ownership group. All agreements among the family must be documented in a legally binding shareholders' agreement, sometimes referred to as a buy-sell agreement or operating agreement.

(See Appendix B for details on creating shareholder agreements.)

This agreement outlines ownership rights, obligations, and restrictions and is signed by all owners after legal counsel review. The agreement addresses issues such as board of director membership; shareholder versus board authority levels for key decisions; owner distribution and dividend policies; capital call requirements; capital expenditure or debt authorization approvals; ownership transfer requirements, rights, and restrictions; termination of family member employment; and other related matters. These agreements should be tailored to your family's needs and be as broad or detailed as desired.

If the conclusion is to retain the family enterprise and ownership goals are defined and aligned, then the additional details for a successful transition can be developed. Of course, each step will require ownership discussions to be certain the overall succession plan meets the ownership's evolving needs and goals.

3. Retirement and Estate Planning

The objective of this section is to achieve certainty that the current generation has both a personal and financial plan for retirement. It encompasses creating purpose, providing adequate financial resources, and structuring a tax-sensitive estate plan.

Retirement can be stressful and at times even scary for the current generation. It represents a significant life transition for them. Their concerns create stresses that often are not voiced. Unfortunately, these silent issues often reduce or prevent the current generation from initiating or participating in the development of succession plans.

Common fears from retirement include the following:

- Lacking purpose ("The business is my life!")
- Dying prematurely ("Jim died soon after he retired!")
- Becoming nobody—losing identity and self-worth ("I am being put out to pasture!")
- Losing standing and respect in the community, the business, or even the family ("No one will need or call me anymore!")
- Worrying that the next generation cannot run the business ("They will fight and ruin *my* business!")

People need to retire to something, not nothing. Some are fine with recreational activities, while others need more purpose. Purpose could be within or outside of the family enterprise, in profit or nonprofit organizations.

Developing a personal retirement plan for current-generation family members, therefore, is an essential step in assuring a healthy and sustainable transition for both the current and next generation.

Unless retiring family members are independently wealthy, part of every retirement plan must include preparing a personal financial plan for each retiring family member. The plan must consider ongoing financial support, the impact of inflation, future health care and long-term living support, travel plans, estate taxes, and charitable giving.

Plans should be agreed upon by all parties to prevent surprises in the future that would create problematic family dynamics or impact the liquidity needs of the family members or the business. The financial plans also should consider risk management provisions, such as life and long-term care insurance.

As part of retirement planning, estate plans often are updated to facilitate ownership transition and overall estate planning. A fundamental issue is to determine how much to leave to various beneficiaries and charities. Tax considerations are important, as financial needs for estate taxes can impact the liquidity needs of the business or the next generation.

For larger estates, engaging an experienced estate planning attorney is well worth the professional fees. Tax savings from proper estate planning can save more family enterprise wealth than several years of excellent operating results. The use of trusts, which complicates your financial affairs, are appropriate for larger estates. Trusts provide opportunities to minimize estate taxes, bypass future-generation estate taxes, and provide funding for charity. They can provide income to the current generation while transferring wealth tax-efficiently to the next generation.

4. Governance Planning

The objective of this section is to establish effective governance for two related but separate entities: the family and the business. Both require objective and accountable governance, but each has different issues to oversee.

Two organizations are needed to govern multigenerational family enterprises properly: *a family council* and *a board of directors*. The family council represents the family. The board of directors represents the owners of the family enterprise, a group that generally does not include the entire extended family.

The family council oversees family matters and needs and is responsible for developing policies for consideration and adoption by those family members who are the owners of the family enterprise.

Family councils connect family members to the family business. They also provide a forum to allow family leadership to be aware of changing family member needs and goals. They are particularly important during generational transition, notably for Gen 3 and later families. These families typically have a larger number of family members and are composed of multiple family branches. Many members are less connected to the family enterprise than were those of the prior generations. As a result, family dynamics can change significantly and quickly if not properly addressed. Additional care is needed to assure that the needs, interests, and concerns of all family members are and continue to be addressed.

In smaller families, the council might include all adult family members. In larger families, representatives are typically selected or elected to represent the extended family ownership.

For the business, the board of directors must evolve as the family and the business grow. "Your parents' board of directors" most likely will not be appropriate to meet the needs of the next generation or the next phase of business development. Thus, upon completion of a new strategic plan (see next section), an assessment must be made of necessary board member skills and experience requirements. The requirements emerging from this assessment should be used to formulate selection criteria for recruiting the next generation's board of directors.

Family councils and boards of directors *must be* professionally managed. They need to be composed of qualified individuals who have a sound understanding of business. Having board members who understand family dynamics is also important. Council and board members should be paid and held accountable for active participation and results.

As needs change with your business and your family, appropriate changes to the council and board should be made as well. Term limits are a best practice and are helpful to create turnover and thus places for new participants.

(See chapters 5 and 6 to learn more about developing proper governance organizations for your family and family enterprise.)

5. Business Strategic Planning

The objective of this section is to encourage careful examination of your business's outlook to develop a strategic plan that meets the next generation's goals.

Many next-generation CEOs adopt the prior generation's business strategies, organization, and general way of running the business. While doing so might appease the prior generation, this practice is a missed opportunity and potentially a gigantic mistake. Business environments change continually, and strategic plans need fresh and objective thinking. Even when prior generations have been very successful, family leadership during the later years often exhibits a low appetite for risk and change. Generational leadership transitions are a ripe time for new direction and an infusion of younger energy.

Prior to beginning a strategic planning process, a CEO needs to communicate to the management team the ownership's goals (from step 2) and the desired management culture—how is management going to work together?

Perhaps resulting from a management consulting background, when I became CEO, I encouraged our management team to challenge *everything* during the transition of our family business. There were no sacred cows. Everybody had a responsibility to generate ideas for any area of the company, not just those where an executive had direct responsibility.

The end result was an aligned management team with new business strategies, a new management culture, specific goals, agreed-upon decision-making guidelines, and performance metrics. These were major changes to the business.

However, the most significant and beneficial change was the creation of an empowered middle and senior management team responsible and accountable to me and ultimately to the owners for results. (A few years later, we empowered our production line workers in a similar manner and received tremendous results from those team members.)

The first step in strategic planning is to evaluate current plans and their appropriateness for meeting present and future needs of the business while also appraising future opportunities. This is a vital step in crafting go-forward strategies. A typical analysis of the business's strengths, weaknesses, opportunities, and threats (SWOT analysis) is an excellent starting point in developing the next generation's strategic plan.

Disruptive technologies, increased competition, new value propositions, and shorter product life cycles impact virtually all businesses. A transition therefore is a good time to develop a new or refreshed business strategy. The process of doing so will provide an impetus for implementing the desired management and governance changes and obtaining the financial resources necessary to realize the future promise of the business. Furthermore, the process will further facilitate management and ownership alignment and support.

6. Risk Assessment and Contingency Planning

The objective of this section is to encourage the board and senior management team to identify and prepare for both the probable and the potential risks that could wreak havoc on your family enterprise.

Business leaders and investors continuously make risk-reward decisions, either formally or informally. A differentiating factor is that most successful companies have excellent risk-reward decision makers.

Risk assessment and management is a critical skill for your board and senior management team. The skills are regularly used to evaluate *recurring and opportunistic-based decisions.* Examples include the following: "Should we acquire this business? Make this investment? Terminate this product, division, or executive? Implement this strategy, marketing project, R&D project, financing, etc.?"

While successful business leaders often are good risk managers, they do not regularly apply these same critical skills when evaluating risks for the *unanticipated*—those "black swan" or once-in-a-generation events. As we all learned from the 2008 Great Recession, unexpected and low-probability risks do occur. They also can have a huge impact on your business and family, through no fault of your own.

With low-probability risks, family owners, boards, and management teams either are unaware of the risks or they adopt a "hope" strategy that something really bad and improbable will not happen. As we all know, "hope" is *not* a strategy!

Examples of unanticipated risks include the following:

- Unexpected death or disability of the CEO or other key executive (e.g., chief marketing officer)
- Loss of an expected refinancing or existing financing of the business
- Bankruptcy or loss of a major customer (i.e., credit risk)
- Loss of a critical supply base
- Physical calamity to plant resulting in business interruption
- Prolonged union strike or labor problems
- Governmental regulatory problems
- Litigation costs and disruption
- Ownership lawsuits or proxy fights

Based on my experience from serving on over twenty-five business and nonprofit boards, I have found most boards do not address *unexpected* risks. Rather, they focus primarily on current business strategies, organizational needs, and financial matters.

Too many families witness firsthand the "surprise" of an unexpected significant event. These events create an untimely and negative impact on the family and the family enterprise. While they may not be preventable, smart risk managers develop and implement written contingency or emergency plans to mitigate the impact of these unlikely events that might occur.

A periodic and careful assessment of unanticipated risks in the family enterprise should be made an essential step in developing a succession plan. Upon completion, the plan should be an agenda item for your board to review and approve so that your family enterprise always has plans in place to address *unlikely* business risks.

Additionally, these plans will help provide new insights that benefit the development of your critical governance, organizational, and financial plans discussed in this chapter.

7. Management Organizational Planning

The objective of this section is to create a management organization that can succeed in implementing the business's strategic plan and meeting the ownership's investment objectives.

As mentioned earlier, too many succession plans are limited just to the selection of the next generation's CEO. While this is a critical decision step, it is by itself inadequate. An effective and successful organizational succession plan should provide for a fully defined management team that can implement the business strategic plan.

The first organizational decision is to determine if a family member or nonfamily member should be the next CEO. A board of directors, or board of advisors, can be very helpful in making this decision and communicating it to the stakeholders.

This decision can be made from a business or a family perspective. The fundamental question is whether the family enterprise's primary focus is to provide management jobs for the family or to maximize shareholder value. While the answer is often some of each, it is worthy of a discussion among the ownership and will help define ground rules for family employment in the business. Once determined, you can build a management team.

The best approach is to determine the specific organizational requirements necessary to *implement* the new strategic plan. You will use those requirements to develop selection criteria to evaluate candidates for various management positions, including that of the CEO.

Both technical and experiential capabilities and qualitative skills, such as fitting in with the family's culture, must be considered. Strong interpersonal skills are always essential in building a management team and maintaining family harmony. As CEO of our family business, I used an outside firm to evaluate candidates' skills to be certain we were creating an effective team that would work well together.

During management transitions, stylistic and culture changes often occur with a new CEO. When I accepted the CEO position of our Gen 3 family business, I was new to the organization. My style was much different from my father's, the Gen 2 CEO. This was in part by design and in part because we were different people! I could not function well by adopting his style nor did I want to replicate it. Times were different, and the CEO job now required a different and more inclusive management approach.[*]

8. Family Leadership Development Planning

The objective of this section is to train and develop the management organization so that family members and others will be able to manage the family enterprise successfully after a generational transition.

A common mistake among my family business clients is a tendency to ignore the serious and ongoing need for management development planning.

Strong, "control-oriented" family business leaders, particularly founders and entrepreneurs, are often not effective (or interested) in

---

[*] My good friend and fellow YPO member Bob Chapman wrote a new book, *Everybody Matters*, which offers transformative lessons on building a new leadership culture. It is well worth reading.

developing future family business leaders. This results in the leaders who follow them being unprepared for or incapable of taking over from the prior generation. This shortcoming is further exacerbated when the size and complexity of the family enterprise has increased significantly over a period of years.

Too often, when the reality of a generational change of management becomes imminent and existing family members are not ready to run the business, the sole conclusion is often that the family *needs* to sell the business.

This decision is often a shock and blow to family members in the next generation who have looked forward to owning and participating in the family business. It is also ironic because so many family business leaders continually state that they are building the business for the next generation.

When succession planning is updated on a regular basis, and particularly prior to a transition, it provides time to develop the next generation of family business leadership and the acceptance of a future transition plan. This reduces or eliminates the panic response that "we must sell the business."

Succession planning in a family business *must* include the cardinal task of developing family members for future leadership, just as a large public corporation must do to assure its perpetuation.

The first step in any organizational development plan is to identify potential leaders, current and future. The second is to determine the actions that can be taken to strengthen and expand the candidates' managerial capabilities and experiences. Examples include the following:

- Having future family leaders run a smaller division of the business or start up a new division;

- Requiring formal education and outside relevant work success prior to joining the family enterprise so expectations for family employment are understood by the future generations;

- Providing training to family management members through an executive MBA program or special purpose management training programs at local business schools;

- Transferring department heads to other departments or divisions in the company to gain broad company experience and demonstrated management competency; or

- Retaining executive coaching consultants or participating in external mentoring and peer learning organizations, such as the Young Presidents' Organization (YPO) or Vistage International.

9. Stakeholder Communications Planning

The objective of this section is to develop communication strategies to be employed during a time of transition to address and inform the many constituents of your family enterprise.

There are many stakeholders in a family enterprise. The first step is to define them. These are examples of typical stakeholders for whom specific communication plans are required or highly desired:

- Family members involved in the business

- Family members not currently involved in the business who might or will be in the future

- Current management team

- Employees, and if unionized, union leadership

- Key customers and suppliers

- The company's professional service providers, including accountants, bankers, and attorneys
- Industry leaders
- Community leaders
- Local and (where relevant) national press

Any communication plan should address the reason for the transition and assure the stakeholders that it has been well planned and will be seamless. A commitment to company values and culture should be reaffirmed. The new CEO should convey appreciation of past support from all stakeholders in the business.

In-person individual or group meetings are preferred, at least for key constituents. Social media, press releases, and letters are typically best treated as supportive, not primary, for your most important constituents—family members, employees, customers, and suppliers.

Information to communicate could include the following:

- Introduction and background of the new CEO.
- Revisions to the board of directors with biographies of new and existing members.
- Revisions to the senior management team with brief biographies of new or key team members.
- Overview of new business strategies and plans.
- Commitment to existing relationships.
- Outreach to any stakeholder desiring additional information or a meeting with the CEO.
- Outreach to business or nonprofit organizations that the company or management members belong to or support.

The initial days of a transition are critical. *All* existing stake-holders will be on high alert to try to determine how the business is changing—for better or for worse!

Working with your management team prior to a transition to create a written 100-day plan is extremely valuable. It will focus management attention on key initiatives and *measurable* results. (100-day plans also work well when acquiring or starting a new business.)

The plan should follow a typical business plan format, with a strong emphasis on communications. Content would include strategy, organization, operations, finance, marketing and sales, administration, and technology.

As the new CEO of our family business, I developed new business strategies supported with detailed business plans to kick off our transition. This created excitement within our ownership and management team and provided a specific focus on short-term accomplishments.

The result was a new culture and method of managing our business with metrics, focus, individual empowerment, and corresponding rewards and recognition. Starting boldly with a sharply defined focus is important in changing from one culture to another.

Our family company transitioned from a sole "in-control" president to an empowered and accountable management team. It required significant changes to the prior generation's organization and way of doing business. The planning process, however, served to knit the family together in a unified mission. The results were well worth the effort.

Summary

Spending the time and effort required for achieving comprehensive succession planning is essential in multigenerational family enterprises. The plan should be in writing and periodically updated as needs and changes occur.

This process not only provides for a successful transition without excessive problematic family dynamics but also produces strong and immediate results that are valued by the prior, current, and future generations of family members.

Perhaps most importantly, it also meets the common goal of passing a successful family enterprise legacy on to each future generation—a goal that is seldom achieved today!

Chapter

EIGHT

Selling Your Family Business

*Understand the far-reaching impacts of selling your family business
and how best to prepare the business and the family for a sale.*

SELLING A FAMILY BUSINESS, particularly a multigenerational business, produces profound impacts on families, some quite unanticipated and undesirable. I know. I sold one of our family's ninety-eight-year-old operating companies as a result of an industry consolidation that provided our family with a deal too good to turn down.

Fortunately, we had another family business that we retained. This business provided a family business for our fourth generation. Even so, selling our main operating company affected our family well beyond monetary returns. Today, for example, we seldom get together as we did in "the good old days" since some of the family members chose not to continue working in the remaining family business.

Family Matters!

Selling your family business is more than just a financial trans-action. You also are selling a way of life. The business provides a strong support system for your family members' egos, emotions, and financial needs *and* their connections with each other. The impact of a sale will affect them for the rest of their adult lives.

People define themselves by their work. "I am a lawyer, busi-ness executive, doctor, etc." Family owners and executives, with their family name over the door, often find their sense of self and their place in the community through their association with the family business. Selling a family business eliminates those valued touchstones of life. There is no longer a family entity to provide its owners with

1. a sense of identity and a purpose ("I run or own XYZ family business");

2. a place to go every day;

3. a loss of family connection (e.g., families rarely see each other as regularly after a sale);

4. a sense of power and control over the family (e.g., default head of the family);

5. regular interaction and camaraderie with fellow associates;

6. community recognition and a sense of prestige in their community;

7. opportunities to join other boards, including nonprofits;

8. predictable and controllable financial support;

9. business perks; and

10. a "safe place" for older members who fear unwanted retirement and want to be considered "in the game"!

These qualitative and often highly emotional issues can significantly impact family members. Family members need to discuss thoroughly whether they are really prepared, *financially and emotionally*, to sell their family business. (In addition, they also need to evaluate objectively whether the business is ready for sale.)

Families considering a sale of the business should take an important and beneficial step early in the process—developing transition plans for each family member active in the business. Creating family investment companies, foundations, and annual reunions are some of the healthy ways to maintain family relationships and provide purpose.

Once these personal factors are considered and addressed, you can focus on the central business tasks that will maximize your financial returns from the sale.

Valuing Your Family Business

Your business outlook and the predictability and reliability of future cash flows are the three main drivers for valuing your business. A common mathematical model for valuing businesses is based on a multiple of free cash flow: earnings before interest, taxes, depreciation, and amortization (EBITDA).

EBITDA x Valuation Multiple = Enterprise Value

Valuation firms use several methodologies to value businesses, such as: *capitalization ("cap") rates* (common for real estate companies); *book value multiples* (common for financial companies); *revenue multiples* (common for growing technology firms); *net book values* (as a secondary consideration); *asset appraisals* to determine downside risk and assets available for financing; and *discounted future cash flows*. Valuation firms often average different valuation methods to finalize their valuation.

An EBITDA-based valuation correlates with several of these other valuation metrics and thus is a simple and an easily computable proxy for family businesses to use in valuing their business.

Business Valuation Model

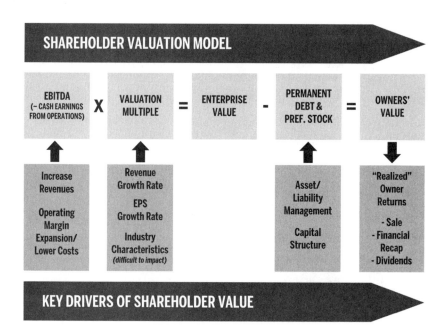

The following describes each component and how the model determines enterprise and equity values:

- *EBITDA*—Pretax operating profits measured before noncash expenses, such as depreciation and amortization. EBITDA differs from net income, which has depreciation and amortization deducted, and from tax paying entities, which have income taxes deducted. EBITDA is a proxy for cash flow from operations (excluding working capital changes).

- *Valuation Multiple*—The valuation multiple is similar to the price/earnings (P/E) multiple used to value public company stocks. To determine the gross value of a business (enterprise value), multiply the valuation multiple times EBITDA.

- *Enterprise Value*—Enterprise value is the value of the entire business's capital structure, which includes the value of permanent debt, preferred stock, and shareholder or owners' equity.

- *Shareholder or Owners' Equity Value*—Owners' equity value is determined by subtracting the business's permanent debt and preferred stock from enterprise value. It represents the value an outside buyer would theoretically pay for your business. Owners' equity is referred to as "stock" in corporations, "membership interests" in limited liability companies, and "partnership interests" in general and limited partnerships.

Best practices include informally valuing your business regularly and including the information in your annual report to family stakeholders.

While an annual valuation assessment is a useful guide for measuring the *performance* of the company, it may conflict with a desire for lower valuations to support estate and gift transfer purposes by family members who are planning a transfer of ownership.

Also, recognize that timing impacts valuations because management cannot affect marketplace factors, which change over time and can have a large impact on EBITDA multiples. Two examples are prevailing interest rates for acquisition financing and strength of demand from buyers for private equity investments.

In valuing a business for sale, owners must be aware that potential buyers evaluate both financial and nonfinancial metrics.

Increasing Shareholder Value

Based on my experience advising and running companies, there always are opportunities to improve shareholder value. To realize them requires a mental stepping away from the day-to-day operating issues that can become all consuming—something too few CEOs take the time to do.

The first step for CEOs is to analyze each element in the business valuation model to determine which "levers" create the greatest benefit. Once assessed, the next step is to determine the probability of implementation success and then the time and resources necessary to realize the benefit.

The final step is to establish a work plan with your management team, specifying priorities, milestones, and accountability assignments.

Whether you sell or keep the family business, focusing on strategic and operational opportunities to improve EBITDA and your EBITDA multiple will prove extremely valuable to the ownership.

Breaking down your business into the detail components that

create value provides a good structure to identify the best opportunities to increase the value of your business. I developed the following operational review road map and have used it many times, both at Deloitte Consulting and with family businesses.

Operational Review Road Map

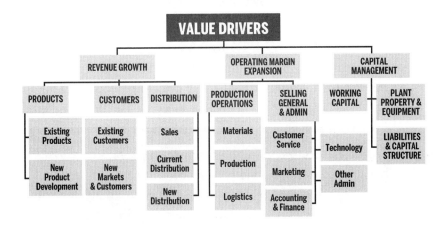

To increase shareholder value, management must concentrate on improving controllable factors, such as the business's revenues, operating margins, growth rates, and capital (asset and liability) management effectiveness.

Changes that increase the EBITDA multiple will produce the greatest increase in company value. For example, increasing your EBITDA multiple from 5X (i.e., five times EBITDA) to 6X generates a 20 percent increase in company value; increasing it to 7X provides a 40 percent increase in company value.

The following financial components present opportunities to increase shareholder value by improving EBITDA and/or the EBITDA multiple.

- **Operating Margins**—Higher gross margin and operating margin businesses support a higher valuation multiple than lower margin businesses. Higher margin businesses provide increased shareholder returns by generating larger operating profits for every incremental dollar of revenues as compared to lower margin businesses. They also can absorb cost increases or margin pressures from competition, thus lowering the business's risk profile.

- **Growth Rates**—Both top-line (i.e., revenues) and bottom-line (i.e., earnings) growth rates impact EBITDA valuation multiples. A higher-growth company will benefit from a higher EBITDA multiple because earnings increase each year from a base year. Buyers pay more for a business whose EBITDA increases every year.

- **Capital Structure**—Capital structure impacts owner value because shareholder value, the amount received by the owners, is reduced by the amount of permanent debt or preferred stock in a company. The following strategies help mitigate capital structure elements that decrease the equity valuation of the business.

- *Working Capital Strategies*—Working capital lines of credit are debt used to finance accounts receivables and inventories. These credit facilities are not considered permanent debt.

  Thus, a simple strategy to increase shareholder value is to (1) decrease accounts receivable and inventories, and (2) increase your working capital line of credit usage to its full extent. Each of these two strategies generates cash. When the cash is distributed to owners (often tax-free in tax pass-through entities), it often does not impact the selling price. That assumes you can demonstrate for a year or two prior to the sale that the company can successfully operate with the reduced working capital. (It did not impact shareholder value on the sale of our family business.)

Note: Working capital targets are typically set in company purchase agreements so that if working capital at closing is different than the specified target, a purchase priced adjustment, up or down, will occur.

- *Fixed Asset Strategies*—Evaluate nonproductive assets to determine whether to keep them based upon their utilization rates, profit generation, and proprietary strategic value. Consider selling nonproductive assets to generate cash, and replace their functions through outsourcing.

- *Real Estate Strategies*—Consider transferring your real estate, including plant and warehouse facilities, to a newly created family-owned real estate entity. This would require the operating company to pay market rent to the new real estate company. The benefit is two fold: (1) it transfers the family wealth represented by real estate in the operating company to a separate real estate entity, potentially providing additional asset protection, and (2) monetizes the positive arbitrage between the valuation metrics of a real estate company versus an operating company.

As an example, real estate companies are valued at a capitalization ("cap") rate, which today for industrial real estate is around 6 percent to 8 percent. (To convert a cap rate to a comparable EBITDA multiple, divide 1 by the cap rate.) A 6 percent cap rate, therefore, converts to a 16.7 EBITDA multiple (1 divided by 0.06), and an 8 percent cap rate converts to a 12.5 EBITDA multiple.

Because operating businesses regularly sell for 5 to 7 times EBITDA, value is created through an arbitrage of valuation metrics. Rental income received by the real estate company will *increase* shareholder value by 12.5 to 16.7 times. The cost of the rental expense to the operating company will *reduce* shareholder value by 5 to 7 times. As a result, the combined companies' shareholder value will increase (and your family wealth may be in two separate asset-protected entities versus one, if structured appropriately).

Types of Buyers

There are two types of buyers of businesses: **financial buyers** and **strategic buyers**.

Financial buyers, such as private equity investors, have a simple goal: buy a business that delivers sustainable cash flows for several years. They *rely* upon the existing business's capabilities as a stand-alone entity, since they do not have an existing company to absorb the business. Accordingly, the business's organization, systems, operations, and customer base need to be strong to continue supporting the business on a stand-alone basis.

Strategic buyers are already operating in your industry, so they may not have the same degree of reliance on your business as would a financial buyer. They can buy businesses and merge them into their existing organization, operations, and systems. They may not be as concerned with your management team and business infrastructure. They also may be able to identify and exploit synergies achievable by merging your business into theirs and thus are able to pay a higher price for your company.

Family businesses should be ready to sell to either type of buyer. Regardless, the sound management practices necessary to sell your business at the best possible price should be employed whether you ultimately sell the business or keep it for multiple generations.

Getting the Business Ready for Sale

To prepare for a future transaction properly, most companies will need at least two years of work. The first year will be to implement changes and the second year to provide time for the changes to show improvement in your financial statements.

While these preparatory initiatives are time consuming, they are necessary to attract the strongest offers from buyers. Most of the initiatives are also important to continue to build the family business for future success.

For financial buyers, such as private equity firms, investment groups, and other companies not in the same industry, you need to take additional steps to demonstrate to them that the business will continue be successful on a stand-alone basis.

The following major areas should be evaluated and, as necessary, improved to prepare your family business for sale (or for long-term multigenerational success):

1. Organization (Management and Labor)

The capabilities and organizational depth of your management team and its relationship with the workforce is a critical concern for prospective buyers. Good relations with unions are important as well, as evidenced by details on wage rates, work rules, work stoppages, safety records, etc.

The quality of your management team is often the most important nonfinancial factor considered by financial buyers. The key positions, such as chief executive officer, chief financial officer, and chief marketing officer, are their starting point. Buyers want to be certain that these positions are filled with high performers who will remain with the business after the sale. Bench strength is also important to demonstrate. You want to show that the company has capable management in place in the event of a loss of a top manager.

For strategic buyers, the management team might be secondary if they plan to consolidate your family business into their own management team. However, your management culture is always important. Buyers want to be certain that your organization will fit with their existing organization, both in terms of management and labor.

One of my initiatives after becoming CEO of our family business was to rebuild the management depth and talent (and change the culture to an empowered management team). Within the first year, we had new positions for the heads of marketing and sales, finance, and operations. We also built bench strength in each area. This resulted in significant new growth and profits and a strong management team that proved valuable when we sold our main operating business eight years later.

2. Financial Reporting and Planning

The financial statements, budget reporting with variance analyses, and management performance reporting are critical to any buyer.

Accuracy, timing of information, and insightfulness of the analyses will either make a buyer comfortable or concerned. Audited financial statements may not be necessary, but accurate financial accounting systems and reporting with validated internal controls and information system backup and recovery systems are extremely important. If this area is not top-notch, it is *imperative* to have it addressed prior to initiating a business sale discussion.

Part of the "hidden test" will be the family business's ability to respond to questions by providing timely and accurate financial information that a buyer might request. A good financial controller or analyst (in addition to the CFO) is a key financial position to include on the management team.

In our family business, we implemented line item budgets for each manufacturing plant, prepared with variance analysis and comparative metrics reported by the tenth day of each month for the prior month. We did the same at the corporate level.

Strong budgeting provided direction to all managers on the results we needed to achieve to meet our business plan. We also provided our equipment operators with daily operating budgets that measured productivity. These reports told them how they were performing and reminded them of the goals that they had helped develop.

3. Strategies, Markets, and Competition

Buyers will increase their valuation of a company when its management team is planning-oriented. The process of developing plans requires a thorough understanding of the business, while the plans themselves provide a clear road map for management.

Growing markets and an attractive industry are helpful, but these factors are not controllable by the family business. However, growth created by capturing more market share, accelerating new product development, cross-selling other products or services to the existing customer base, and expanding distribution channels provide a growing market to a buyer.

In general, a broad customer base and product line is more appealing than a concentration of a large percentage of your business in a few customers or products. If needed, implementing product and customer diversification strategies will be valuable.

Your competitive position is another key factor in a buyer's analysis. Businesses possessing strong barriers to entry or difficulty for existing customers to switch to another supplier are highly regarded by buyers. In addition, maintaining lower cost structures, pricing dominance in your markets, strong product value propositions, controlled supply bases, and multiyear sales contracts are other means to demonstrate confidence that the business is safe and well positioned for the future.

When relevant, proprietary technologies and intellectual property patents provide additional assurance to buyers.

4. Profitability and Growth Rates

A key consideration in any buyer's assessment of your business is the probability that future cash flows, profitability, and growth rates will remain attractive *after* an acquisition.

From a financial perspective, their investment is based upon projecting future cash flows of the business. Your valuation and chances for successfully selling your business increase to the extent that your cash flows and profits are growing, are not very volatile, and bear only a minimal risk of declining,

In preparing for a potential sale, you should evaluate profit margins by customer, by product line or product, and by distribution channel—any sophisticated buyer will do it if you don't.

Regardless, this type of information should be reported to your management team regularly to identify areas that need improvement. For example, unprofitable or low profit margin business can be detrimental to the overall company performance evaluation. When noted, management can address deficiencies through cost cutting, pricing increases, value engineering, or, if necessary, elimination of the sale.

In our family business, our highest-volume product was sold to our largest customer—not an uncommon dynamic. However, within a few months after I joined our family business, the customer reengineered our product, resulting in the elimination of most of our profit margin.

While it was dicey to address, we were able to renegotiate a new arrangement, thanks to good financial reporting on our overall customer profitability. The solution was not what had initially been proposed (a raise in our pricing!); rather it was an initiative to develop approximately five times more business with this customer, thus allowing us to make sufficient money on the new business to more than compensate for the low margins of the original business. It worked out very well for us and our customer.

5. Fixed Assets (Plant, Property, and Equipment)

Buyers will carefully examine your facilities from two perspectives: (1) Are your operations well organized and managed, properly maintained, and competitive in terms of cost, quality, and technology? (2) Is there excess capacity to support additional output (i.e., free capacity that when utilized is not reflected in your current financial statements revenues and profits)?

Additionally, consider whether any significant capital expenditures will be necessary in the near term to support the business. If so, they could trigger a reduction in the business valuation.

6. Risk Management

In general, buyers will be evaluating the riskiness of acquiring your business during their due diligence phase. All the items discussed above will be assigned a risk assessment.

As a separate due diligence step, longer-term contracts, existing financing terms and conditions, product warranties, known or potential contingent liabilities of any nature, and governmental regulatory risk will be evaluated.

As the third-generation CEO of our family business, I had our management team evaluate our business using these principles during my first six months of employment. In leading this effort, it was helpful to join the company with the benefit of fresh eyes and eleven years of professional management consulting experience.

We included several of the above-listed recommendations in my first business plan. Our management team implemented them over the following two years and created significant new shareholder value.

Eight years thereafter, we received two unsolicited and unique offers to buy one of our two family businesses from strategic buyers seeking to consolidate our industry. While our family never expected to sell our business, our prior initiatives and track record of growth generated a strong valuation from these prospective buyers that was too significant to turn down.

In addition, our performance led to opportunities for our entire management team to be retained by the public company that chose to acquire us, a wonderful benefit that kept our team together. In addition, we retained our other family business for the fourth generation.

Financial Headwinds of Selling Your Business

I confess, nonetheless, to retaining a strong bias against selling a family business. I believe family businesses should not be sold unless there are overwhelmingly compelling business or family reasons for doing so.

From the business perspective, a dismal outlook, hopefully identified before being displayed in your financial statements, would be a good reason to sell, *if* it cannot be fixed. Many causes can create that dismal outlook: industry characteristics, competitive positioning, ending product life cycles, inadequate human resource capabilities, and declining or static growth outlook, among others.

Simply put, if your business cannot thrive and grow, it most likely should be sold.

There are also business structural issues that would suggest a sale is a good strategy. These include declining or minimal cash generation, significant additional risk-laden capital requirements, underperforming shareholder returns on assets, unacceptable risk outlook, or a lack of human capital to perpetuate the business.

Family considerations are a separate reason that businesses are sold. For example, a sale may be necessary when the ability to divide up one's estate as desired is not possible, or heirs have differing needs and desires. Intractable and problematic family dynamics may make continued coexistence in a business untenable. In addition, when management is composed of some family members but excludes many other family owners, the alignment of family goals can be impossible, and sale of the business is the only reasonable resolution.

The following typical complaints are NOT acceptable reasons for selling a company. They all can be prevented and addressed, if there is a proper family and business management desire, time, and dedication to do so.

- "No one is capable to take over from me."
- "We need liquidity for estate taxes."
- "We can't agree upon the direction of the company."
- "We don't have enough capital to make necessary investments."
- "Nobody wants to work in the business."
- "We can't choose a CEO because we have multiple children employed in the business."

The singular most important problem with selling your family business is that doing so nearly always destroys family wealth.

The math is simple: the proceeds of the sale after taxes leave you with less money, which, when reinvested in publicly traded securities, returns lower yields than your family business.

Of course, there are rare times and market conditions when a family can sell its business at a significantly greater value than it might normally be worth. In those situations, the opportunity may be too attractive to turn down and would be economically wise to accept. In those rare situations, prior to accepting an offer, be certain to understand the after-tax impact on family cash flow and wealth accumulation that the sale will produce.

Tax aspects of a family business sale are critical to the amount of net proceeds the family receives from a sale. Before proceeding with the *idea* of selling your business, engage legal and tax counsel to evaluate the income and estate taxation and deal structure issues associated with a sale. These are complicated considerations, but they can have a profound effect on the level of financial rewards you will gain from selling your business.

Common issues include understanding the impact on estate and gift taxes and plans, tax basis step-ups, ordinary income taxes, recapture taxes, capital gain taxes, tax-free exchanges, and asset-versus-entity sales options.

The following table illustrates the impact of taxation on a business sale. It is a simple example to display how family wealth *decreases* the day after a sale.

SALE OF BUSINESS ECONOMICS

Company EBITDA	$5,000,000
EBITDA Valuation Multiple	6X
Enterprise Value	$30,000,000
Less: Permanent Debt/Preferred Stock Units	-0-
Company Selling Price	$30,000,000
Transaction Costs (Legal, Tax, Closing) at 1%	$300,000
Net Shareholder Proceeds before Taxes	$29,700,000
Federal and California Taxes[1]	$8,910,000
Net Shareholder Sales Proceeds	$20,790,000
% Loss of Family Wealth ($20.8MM/$30.0MM)	31%

(1) A 30% estimated tax rate is a reasonable approximation for illustrative purposes. The estimate is based on current maximum marginal tax rates of 20% for long-term capital gains, 3.8% for net investment income,

13.3% for California income, and assuming a 25% tax basis in the company equity and no recapture taxes.

Family Wealth Impact

The preceding example illustrates how a family business that generated $5 million in EBITDA is left with net after-tax cash proceeds of $20.8 million to reinvest. To be comparable, presale EBITDA should probably be reduced by $500K to allow for capital expenditures resulting in an adjusted presale EBITDA of $4.5 million. That is the amount of pretax free cash flow available for shareholder distributions.

Thus, from an investment perspective, $4.5 million in pretax cash flow was "sold" for $20.8 million in after-tax sales proceeds.

As a simple illustration of impact, the family needs to generate a 22 percent pretax return on investment for the business's sales proceeds to generate the same amount of pretax cash flow the business was generating previously (i.e., $4.5 million divided by $20.8 million).

With a typical 60 percent equity/40 percent fixed-income portfolio, investment advisors estimate a 7 percent pretax annual return in today's market. At a 7 percent return, the family would receive $1.5 million in pretax cash flow (7 percent times $20.8 million). Even with a 10 percent return, these financial returns are comparatively devastating.

By selling the family business, the family experiences a $3 million reduction in annual cash flow (i.e., $1.5 million versus $4.5 million), and a loss of investment capital due to taxes of around $9 million (i.e., $30 million versus $20.8 million).

The math is simple, and the conclusions are consistent for varying sales transactions.

In this illustration, the business has $5 million in EBITDA and is valued at five, six, and seven times EBITDA multiples. The implied business return of the family for a five-multiple valuation is 20 percent (i.e., 1 divided by 5). After the payment of income taxes from the sale of the business, however, the family now has only 69 percent of the sales proceeds to reinvest. It therefore needs to produce a return that is 145 percent greater (1 divided by 0.69) than the existing family business returns—a feat that is improbable.

BREAK-EVEN RETURNS AFTER FAMILY BUSINESS SALE			
Factor	5X Multiple	6X Multiple	7X Multiple
Investment Returns from Existing Family Business			
EBITDA	$5 MM	$5 MM	$5 MM
Owners' Value	$25 MM	$30 MM	$35 MM
"Implied" Business ROI	20.0%	16.7%	14.3%
Equivalent Returns Required After Selling Business			
Net Sales Proceeds	$17.33 MM	$20.80 MM	$24.27 MM
Break-Even	28.9%	24.0%	20.6%

While the sale of the business offers an increased degree of prudence in that it provides a diversified portfolio and greater liquidity, the price paid for this benefit is high. The family now receives only one-third to one-half of the cash flow previously provided by the family business. In addition to losing cash flows, family members working in the family business may also have to forfeit their salaries, benefits, and perks, unless retained by the new owner with similar remuneration.

In conclusion, the taxation penalty from selling your business is a permanent loss of investment capital. Why? After the sale (and taxes), you now have approximately *one-third less* of your original capital available to you for reinvestments. And you will reinvest these funds at much lower investment return rates than your family business provided.

Your overall wealth never catches up. In fact, each year your family wealth portfolio and cash flow fall further behind.

My bottom line: a healthy family business with good prospects is your best vehicle for creating income and preserving wealth in today's investment environment—second to none!

Final Caveat

I recognize that liquidity and investment diversification from a family wealth management perspective is valuable. This can be accomplished while still growing a family business through proper planning that extends over a five-to-seven-year time horizon.

(This topic and other family business wealth management issues are further addressed in chapters 9 and 10.)

Chapter

NINE

Avoiding the Family Business
Wealth Evaporation Trap

*Manage your family business as an investment to improve
shareholder returns and meet both business and individual needs.*

MOST CONSERVATIVELY MANAGED MULTIGENERATIONAL family
businesses unwittingly *destroy shareholder wealth* every year, despite
their leaders' best intentions.

Unfortunately, this wealth evaporation does not show up as a line
item on the company's financial statements, so it is both unrecognized and perpetuated for years in many family businesses.

Family businesses fall into this "wealth evaporation trap" by virtue
of three management flaws, which, while easily reversible, are potentially devastating to the owners if not recognized and addressed.

- First, leaders manage their business with a narrow and limited perspective, viewing it only as an "operating entity." They fail to consider that the company is a "financial investment"—in fact, often the largest part of the owning family's overall wealth portfolio.

- Second, leaders fail to recognize the critical difference between company return on equity (ROE) and shareholder-realized ROE—that is, the difference between *created and realized shareholder returns.*

- Third, leaders fail to understand that their overly conservative financial management results in poor stewardship of the family's overall wealth, exposing family members to unrecognized risks, lower long-term investment returns, and diminished liquidity.

The inevitable consequence, even in very successful companies, is the silent and unseen evaporation of family wealth, often over a single generation. These same flaws also create problematic family dynamics when the financial results eventually do not meet either business or family shareholder needs.

Fortunately, by evaluating and implementing the proper short-term and longer-term alternative strategies, the company's management and board of directors can begin to resolve these problems very quickly.

Unfortunately, though, most boards pay minimal attention to two of their most important and critical functions: (1) maximizing *realized* shareholder value and (2) protecting shareholders' investment by managing risk. Thus, they fail to exercise an essential part of their legal and fiduciary responsibilities. My experiences as a member of fifteen different business boards affirm that these issues seldom even make it to the board's meeting agenda.

Retaining cash is appropriate at certain times, such as for risky or high-growth business environments. However, until cash or other assets are distributed to shareholders and thus "realized," returns are zero! The impact of 0 percent returns in the early years of an investment significantly reduces the magnitude of cumulative shareholder returns over the longer term.

Until shareholders receive cash, they have nothing more than an unrealized stock gain. Yet they have been exposed over the years to business and financial risks similar to those of owning any other illiquid investment.

With public company investments, shareholders can realize value on any day simply by selling their stock. Private company shareholders do not have this option. Rather, their investments lie trapped inside the sealed vault of a privately owned family business, with no meaningful options for sale.

Given this distinction, private companies must act to expand their focus beyond just *creation* of shareholder value to include *realization* of shareholder value.

Shareholder Wealth Evaporation

Shareholder wealth evaporates in privately held businesses in many ways:

1. Time value of money

The delay in distributing cash returns to shareholders generates a significant reduction in overall returns due to the time value of money and inflation. Waiting for a future liquidity event, such as a sale of the business, is costly from an investment return perspective.

Unfortunately, family businesses often treat shareholders as family members rather than investors. However, when a family business recognizes this dynamic and acts to shift its focus to treating shareholders as investors, the leadership can make different and more salutary decisions. These, in turn, bring improved realized returns and, as a complementary benefit, improved family dynamics.

2. Working capital management

Many conservatively managed businesses shy away from corporate debt. They thus fail to manage working capital properly—that is, accounts receivables, inventories, and payables—by accumulating an abundance of retained capital. This misuse of the family business's equity capital results in poor stewardship of a family's wealth.

For example, a business can establish a working capital line of credit today for an interest cost of about 4 percent. By self-funding working capital with retained earnings, the family is making the unconscious decision to "invest" shareholder equity capital in an investment returning a mere 4 percent! This is a common example of why shareholder wealth evaporates over time. The misappropriation of equity capital also impacts the amount of funds available for business reinvestment, thus hurting future growth.

3. Capital structure

Even conservatively managed businesses should have an appropriate level of debt to support the enterprise. A no-debt or low-debt policy for all but high-risk businesses produces substandard shareholder returns due to the lack of financial leverage on the balance sheet.

I have worked with several companies that proudly report they have no debt and have excess cash balances in the company. The result, however, is that they earn only negligible returns on their cash and expose family wealth to lawsuits and other unforeseen risks.

Tax-efficient transfer of excess cash into special purpose entities provides additional asset protection, greater liquidity to individual shareholders, and better diversification of the family's wealth portfolio.

4. Business management focus

Too many privately held businesses focus solely on the income statement—revenues, costs, and profits. When management is not disciplined about generating cash and realizing shareholders returns, it makes decisions that destroy shareholder value.

Examples include unjustifiable capital investments, poor working capital management, substandard cost controls, inadequate product or customer margins, and a financially sloppy management culture. When both profits and cash are central, management makes better decisions.

Cash is said to be king, but *shareholder-realized cash* is the true king!

5. Unrecognized tail risks

Shareholder value retained in the business is exposed to many tail risks that aren't recognized or sufficiently acknowledged by family leadership. Shareholders are not rewarded for assuming these risks.

Examples include declining future economic cycles, new competition with better products, loss of key customers or suppliers, loss of key executives, new governmental regulation, product liability claims, and problematic family dynamics in future generations that hurt the business.

In addition, uncontrollable economic factors, such as interest rates, valuation multiples, and tax rates, can diminish shareholder value. The business economic cycle is still a reality; to wit, the Great Recession of 2008 destroyed shareholder value for many privately owned (and publicly owned) businesses—some irretrievably—at no fault of management in many cases.

Realizing Shareholder Returns

Since realizing shareholder value requires cash or other asset distributions, family enterprise CEOs and their boards need to implement strategies that generate current and future cash flow for their shareholders. There are three primary strategies to consider:

- **Recurring cash distributions** derived from ongoing operating profits plus depreciation and amortization (noncash costs), less current or planned capital expenditures.

- **One-time or periodic cash distributions** derived from improvements in working capital management, restructuring of the business's capital structure, and tax-efficient distributions of assets; an example of the latter would be the sale and leaseback of real estate used by the business.

- **Cash distribution from sale of the business** made possible or enhanced by taking steps that increase the company's valuation before sale and maximize the net proceeds after taxes.

The goal is always to increase shareholder-realized returns while minimizing the exposure to risks. Another way of saying this is "optimizing risk-adjusted returns," a common investment management principle.

A strategy of selling your family business can be costly from a realized return on investment perspective. The taxes from a business sale consume part of the family business equity that is available to reinvest. In addition, reinvestment options often generate lower returns than the family business. The end result is that the family has *less funds to invest in assets with lower returns.*

This means, simply, an inevitable and significant evaporation of family wealth and recurring cash flows. In fact, over time, the gap between the family business's presale returns and those from the reinvested proceeds of the sold business widens dramatically. *(See chapter 8 for additional discussions addressing the sale of a family business.)*

Therefore, a strategy of *partially* distributing family business wealth creation to shareholders on an ongoing basis is typically the best option. This strategy maximizes shareholder-realized returns, improves shareholder liquidity and investment diversification, and reduces exposure to tail risks.

There are exceptions, such as when high-growth companies make an informed decision to retain equity capital in their business to support significant growth opportunities. In those situations, the rewards are often worth the risks; however, when growth slows, wealth realization becomes an important strategic issue.

Client Case Study

My client was a $100 million manufacturing company that was owned by several Gen 2 family shareholders. The business had experienced significant growth through acquisitions, new products, and expanded distribution, both domestically and internationally. By all factors, it was a very successful family business.

Prior to transitioning leadership to Gen 3, the CEO began addressing his family's overall family wealth management strategies, which included estate planning and investment portfolio management.

As an advisor, my first step was to define the family's wealth to include both their traditional investments and the market value of the family business. Many family businesses consider their stock, bond, and real estate portfolios as their "investments" and their family business as their "operating entity." This distinction distorts the view of a family's wealth portfolio and can lead to poor stewardship of family wealth. Fortunately, this was not the case with this client.

Our client had a typical asset allocation where the family business represented a large concentration of wealth as depicted in the chart below. This resulted in an illiquid and undiversified wealth portfolio.

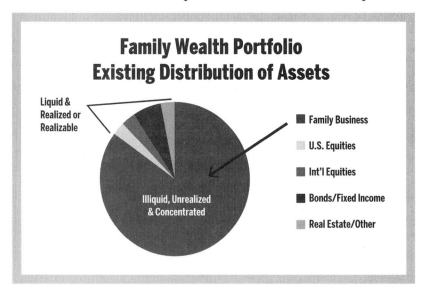

Fortunately, this situation can typically be corrected over time and better meet family wealth management needs *without* constraining the family business. It requires a commitment by family leadership to diversify the family wealth portfolio through distributing trapped family business equity to the owners so that the distributions can be re-invested into other asset classes (see the chart below). This produces a more diversified and asset protected family wealth portfolio.

An additional benefit is the wealth portfolio can support both the business *and* the individual needs and goals of a diverse ownership group by allowing family owners to opt-in or opt-out of various new investments external to the family business.

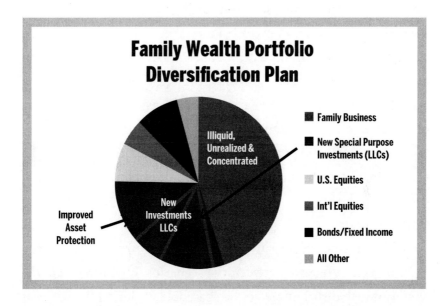

With this client, the first step was to develop financial models to determine the business's future capital requirements and ability to generate cash flow distributions to the owners (without compromising future business results). To test the feasibility, I worked with the business's CFO to evaluate two alternative shareholder distribution strategies to determine the impact of each on the business and the family's overall wealth portfolio.

The company's business plan required capital to support a projected sales growth of 10 percent per year, resulting in sales increasing from $100 million to $236 million over the ten-year projection period. Our model projected a sale of the business at the end of Year 10 for both scenarios to provide an end termination value for comparative purposes.

In scenario 1, annual operating cash flow was retained in the business to provide capital for growth; additional funds were borrowed, as needed, to provide additional growth capital. In Year 5, when operating cash flow exceeded capital investment requirements, the debt was paid off, and any remaining cash flow was distributed to the shareholders. During Year 6 through Year 10, all operating cash flows in excess of annual capital investment requirements were distributed to the shareholders.

In scenario 2, 100 percent of operating cash flows were distributed annually to the shareholders. Bank debt provided all capital for growth. Debt levels over the ten-year period remained within financing norms, reaching a maximum debt/EBITDA (i.e., earnings before interest, tax, depreciation, and amortization) ratio of 2.5 times.

The main difference between the scenarios was the *amount and timing* of cash distributions to the shareholders during the ten-year planning horizon based on a strategy of retaining versus distributing annual cash flows as displayed in table 6.

Table 6. Client Case Study Results

DISTRIBUTE OPERATING CASH FLOWS FOR SUPERIOR SHAREHOLDER RETURNS

(in USD Millions)	Scenario 1 Retain Cash	Scenario 2 Distribute Cash
Year 1–Enterprise Value	$65	Same
Annual Revenues–Year 1	$100	Same
Annual Revenues–Year 10	$236	Same
Cumulative Cash Received through Year 9	$22	$83
Cumulative Cash Received through Year 10 (after company sale)*	$155	$161
% Cumulative Cash Received through Year 9	14%	52%
NPV at 10% of Cash Distributions	$62	$79
10-Year Owner's Internal Rate of Return	13.3%	19.1%

*Due to timing difference of reinvested cash flows received by shareholders.

The different results from the modeling of the two scenarios were significant. Scenario 2 (annually distributing operating cash flow) was far superior in terms of shareholder returns, liquidity, and at-risk capital exposure than scenario 1 (retaining operating cash flow).

Specifically, scenario 2 produced a six-percentage-point increase of annualized returns on shareholder equity—from 13.3 percent to 19.1 percent. Net present value (at a 10 percent discount rate of the cash flow streams) grew from $62 million to $79 million. And, by the ninth year, the shareholders received over 50 percent of their total projected cash for the entire ten-year planning horizon, after including the expected cash from the sale of the business.

These projected annual cash distributions of operating earnings would generate significant family liquidity to meet various family needs and the ability to begin a wealth diversification program. As a result, the family would not have to sell their family business to meet current or future liquidity needs and be able to maintain their family enterprise for future generations.

Family Wealth Road Map

Developing a *family wealth realization plan* is a complex and time-consuming activity. It should provide a road map to determine the optimum way to realize business wealth over time while meeting both business and family shareholder needs and objectives. When properly implemented, it will serve family shareholders more effectively by

- increasing realized internal rates of return and family member liquidity and decreasing exposures to tail risks;
- increasing family wealth asset protection and diversification;
- improving family stakeholder satisfaction and family dynamics;
- introducing better financial management disciplines into the business;
- providing alternative investments to individual family members to meet their individual investment objectives and tolerance for risk more precisely; and
- facilitating tax efficient business wealth transfer and estate planning.

Creating a multidisciplinary team of senior company executives and external professionals experienced in finance, business operational assessment, wealth management, and taxes and estate planning is important. While there are significant benefits, there are risks in terms of protecting the business's financial needs and understanding the tax or legal consequences of various implementation plans. The primary steps in the road map are as follows:

1. Business operational and financial review—Evaluating the business's future cash flow generation capability, sustainability, and volatility, in addition to its capital needs. The goal is to determine the amount of free cash flow available for tax-effective distributions over the following five years.

2. Family needs assessment and wealth management review—Understanding and specifying the individual and overall family's financial objectives and evaluating the family's wealth portfolio, inclusive of the family business asset.

Family dynamics problems are often uncovered during this phase and need to be addressed so that individual family needs do not undermine the future survival of the business. For example, clients where an individual family member's business holdings represent over 75 percent of his or her individual net worth is typically not an ideal situation. This requires additional planning to develop plans that meet both individual and overall family needs.

3. Capital structure review—Rationalizing current working capital, overall business capital structures, and existing shareholder distribution strategies. Business needs, always of upmost importance, are evaluated along with shareholder objectives and needs.

The goals are to meet the current and future capital requirements of the business and to develop strategies to increase *realized* shareholder value through one-time or recurring shareholder distributions.

The team needs to evaluate a variety of options, such as recapitalizing the business through debt or equity transactions; sale-leaseback transactions (real estate, major equipment); spinning off noncore assets into separate asset-protected companies; selling underutilized assets and replacing them by outsourcing; and improving working capital management. In any of these types of transactions, it is imperative to have tax counsel review the tax impact.

4. Shareholder distributions and wealth management planning— Preparing a five-year financial plan for the business and for the family's wealth portfolio.

The project team needs to develop financial models to test various scenarios to determine which plan best supports the business while meeting overall family wealth management investment return objectives.

A large cushion of conservatism, including mandatory annual reviews and modifications of implementation plans based on actual business results and fresh assessments of the economic outlook is recommended.

Under specific conditions, transferring distributions into a separately managed "standby" special purpose entity (SPE) that can be better aligned to meet individual owner goals is the best course of action.

This standby SPE, with a different board than the operating company, can lend funds to the main operating business, guarantee loans, and provide asset protection by holding assets outside of the operating company. An extra benefit is that the assets of the SPE can be protected from exposure to creditors of the main family business operating entity, if set up and managed appropriately.

5. Wealth transfer and asset protection planning—Projects of this nature often lead into gift and estate planning.

Estate planning attorneys' narrow focus on taxes, wealth transfer strategies, and asset protection often miss the important issues that impact family business longevity and overall wealth management. A more holistic and goals-driven approach addressing succession plans, governance, and family dynamics is required.

Plans need to be tailored to meet the goals and objectives of the individual stakeholders, the overall family's wealth (evaluated from an investment portfolio perspective), and the "golden goose"—the family business.

Best of Both Worlds

In summary, private companies have the benefit of longer time horizons for performance measurement than public companies do. They do not have the pressures of public companies to produce ever-increasing quarterly earnings, a blessing and a curse. Because public companies focus on delivering shareholder value, they tend to do a better job on this essential measure.

Private companies need to up their game on this objective. Once they do so, private companies will have the best of both worlds.

Chapter

TEN

Perpetuating Multigenerational Family Wealth

*Understand the strong headwinds that destroy family
wealth, and learn the best strategies to mitigate them.*

MANY FAMILIES DESIRE TO perpetuate some or all of their family's
wealth for the benefit of future generations. Their typical first action
to accomplish this goal is to engage an estate-planning attorney,
who, myopically, addresses only estate and gift tax avoidance.

However, while taxation planning for generational wealth
transfers is essential, related issues need to be addressed as well to
protect and increase the value of a family's wealth for succeeding
generations. Among these are investment management policies,
current- and future-generation wealth creation strategies, and family
spending protocols (i.e., consumption of wealth).

Investment management for any family requires *astute* shepherding of the wealth portfolio of family members, namely stocks and bonds, real estate, and their other holdings in addition to the family business. Investment returns, family spending rates, management fees, income taxes, inflation, correlation volatility with other assets, and estimated growth rates all impact the degree of success in wealth preservation and must be monitored and managed carefully.

Equally critical, families also must manage their family business (often their largest asset) as an *investment*, much as they would any other investment. As discussed in the prior chapter, conservative family business leaders often are not good stewards of family business wealth, namely because of an inbred aversion to debt capital and a strong desire to accumulate cash in the business.

Improper allocation and management of the family business capital will destroy family wealth, as it would for any other investment over time.

Often, families choose to sell their business to provide liquidity and create a more diversified investment portfolio. Selling the family business, however, often reduces family wealth to about *two-thirds of the family business's original selling price*, after the payment of capital gain taxes, income taxes, and transaction costs.

Coupled with the comparatively paltry investment returns available in the public markets, the family winds up with less money to reinvest and lower investment return rates. Not a good strategy for wealth perpetuation!

Several headwinds, described below, make perpetuating family wealth for future generations extremely difficult. Taking certain steps can mitigate these headwinds but not eliminate them.

An excellent mitigation strategy is to cultivate *wealth creators* for each future generation by providing succeeding family members with a broad education, personal financial management training, and other relevant experiences that will provide them with the ability to maintain and create multigenerational wealth.

The Hard Economics

Four strong headwinds erode family wealth. They can be easily remembered by using my acronym, FIST.

Consumption of Family Wealth

- **F**—the number of *family* units supported by the family's wealth
- **I**—*inflation*, the "silent killer" that erodes wealth over time

- **S**—the *spending* rate expressed as a percent of assets that the family consumes

- **T**—*taxes*—income, capital gain, estate, and gift

FIST often shocks families of wealth when they are confronted with the real impact of these four elements. While these concepts are easy to understand when defined and examined, the degree of their collective consumption of a family's wealth is staggering.

Number of Family Units Impact on Family Wealth (F)

The concept is simple. Gen 1 starts a family business composed of one family unit. Gen 1 has two children, creating two additional family units. Gen 2 has two children each, creating four more family units. From Gen 1 to Gen 4, there could be an *eight fold* increase in family units sharing the wealth of the family enterprise.

If parents have more than two children, the increase is even greater. In addition, because people now are living longer, it is common for two or three generations to be supported by a family's wealth.

The following chart depicts how the number of family units increases in each generation.

Reduction of Wealth per Family Unit as Family Growth Increases over Time

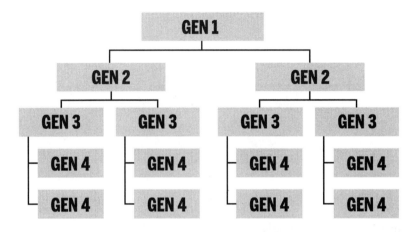

Family grows from one in Gen 1 to eight in Gen 4
with only two children per parent

Inflation Impact on Family Wealth (I)

Inflation's compounding feature over time significantly reduces a family's real wealth—that is, wealth measured in *real dollars*. Real dollars represent true buying power. As an example, at 3 percent inflation, the value of a $1 today is worth $0.74 in ten years and $0.55 in twenty years. From a macro perspective, a $50 million investment portfolio in a 3 percent inflation environment would lose $1,500,000 of real value purchasing power in a year.

Inflation is rightly deemed the "silent killer." It has significant impact and is rarely quantified or reported in investment or financial statements. Thus, it is seldom acknowledged and properly addressed as *a significant long-term loss of family wealth*.

Furthermore, next-generation family members, who often are more risk adverse than the wealth creator's generation, do not want to lose what has been bestowed upon them. Many translate their sense of stewardship into a policy of low-risk (and therefore low-return) investing. Trust companies often perpetuate similar conservative investment strategies to avoid losing money (and trust fees) and risking exposure to litigation.

Unfortunately, low-risk investing coupled with inflation results in returns that fail to maintain multigenerational wealth.

Inflation Impact on $1 Over Time

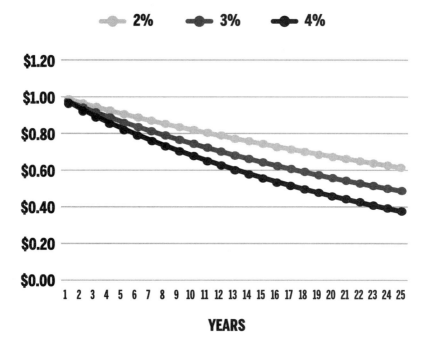

YEARS

Spending Impact on Family Wealth (S)

Spending is determined by the amount of a family's wealth distributed to the family stakeholders each year. It should be evaluated as a rate, based on the family's annual consumption of family wealth expressed as a *percentage of investable assets*. It is the most controllable factor of all the FIST elements. However, it can be extremely difficult to manage because individual family members often have sharply divergent financial circumstances and needs.

For example, a CEO with a large compensation package might support low spending rates (i.e., distributions to the family) to preserve assets for his or her children and grandchildren. Another family member, however, may be a teacher with a low salary and want higher spending rates by the family business so he or she can better fund a child's educational expenses. This creates a paradox—each family member is making the best decision for his or her individual circumstances but *not* for the *collective* family. This dilemma can impact the wealth available for future generations.

If, however, the current family leadership chooses to *reduce* spending rates for the current generation as a means to preserve wealth for future generations, different problems may arise. Families come to rely on regular and consistent distributions to plan their financial affairs. The board tends to conform by requiring the maintenance of those distributions for the foreseeable future to accommodate those expectations.

Similarly, caution must be taken before *increasing* distributions to ensure that they can be continued at the increased level for the foreseeable future. When excess funds are available to distribute, a one-time special distribution works best because it does not impact family members' future expectations. One way to "insure" the ability to maintain a level of family stakeholder distributions is to retain two years' worth of future distributions in cash reserves.

A best practice for management is to communicate distribution expectations annually to its family owners for the upcoming two- or three-year period. This approach provides adequate visibility so that families can plan their personal affairs with the assurance of cash distributions for a few years.

To determine optimum spending rates, management must evaluate the portfolio's after-tax income as a percentage of assets. Income should include realized and unrealized income. To maintain real wealth, without accounting for the needs of future family members, income must be balanced with spending, taxes, and inflation costs. This formula will prevent the current generation from consuming family wealth.

This spending calculation is easy to compute. The challenge is to try to ensure that it will it meet the current needs of the entire family. Expressing these elements as a percentage of assets is a recommended way to communicate the results to the family.

Taxation Impact on Family Wealth (T)

The biggest spending partner in a family is probably Uncle Sam. When adding up federal and state taxes, even after the tax reductions in 2018, a tremendous amount of annual investment return is eliminated.

The following illustrates the impact of taxes on investment returns for a California family:

- Size of family wealth portfolio
  $50,000,000

- Annual pretax investment returns of 7%
  $3,500,000

For illustrative purposes, our model assumed returns were 100% passive income and realized at 50% capital gains, 15% qualified dividends, 35% ordinary income tax rates, and excludes gift or estate taxes and the $10,000 limited state tax deduction.

- Income taxes:

  » Federal income tax at 37% on $1,225,000 ordinary income **($453,250)**

  » Federal income tax on qualified dividends and capital gains at 20% on $2.275 million **($455,000)**

  » Net investment income tax at 3.8% on $3.5 million of income over $250,000 threshold **($123,500)**

  » California income tax at 13.3% on $3.5 million **($465,500)**

  » Total Income Tax **($1,497,250)** (equivalent to 43% of income and 3% of investable assets)

- After tax investment return **$2,002,750**
- Real dollar loss from 2.75% inflation **($1,375,000)**
- Remaining investment return (available for spending without reducing real wealth; equivalent to 1.3% of wealth portfolio) **$627,750**

After 2.75 percent inflation, only 1.3 percent of the wealth portfolio is available for spending if the goal is to maintain family wealth (without considering increases in the number of family units being supported in the future.)

The FIST Knockout Punch

The following model illustrates the impact of all four FIST elements (number of family units, inflation, spending, and taxes) on multigenerational wealth.

A model was created using the same inputs expressed as a percentage of assets used in the taxation section (7 percent income; 2.75 percent inflation; 3 percent taxes), plus a 3 percent spending rate. These assumptions are reflective of current public market investment returns and tax rates. While simple to communicate and understand, the model depicts a recurring elimination of family wealth.

Wealth Perpetuation Model

Element	Percentage of Assets
• Income generation	7.00%
• Income taxes (no estate taxes)	(3.00%)
• Inflation	(2.75%)
• Spending	(3.00%)
• Real $ Annual Gain/(Loss)	(1.75%)

To introduce the family unit component (F), assume Gen 1 is the sole stakeholder until the fifth year, when two children are included as stakeholders. In the tenth year, Gen 1 is no longer a stakeholder, and Gen 2 along with both of Gen 2's two children become stakeholders, resulting in six family member units.

The future impact on available spending in *real dollars* per family unit is devastating. At a 3 percent spending rate, available cash flow in real dollars per family unit is reduced from $1,500,000 in Year 1 to $214,000 in Year 10, a meager 15 percent of the Gen 1's original cash flow per family member.

Even with a modest 3 percent spend rate, the family wealth portfolio does not retain its value, decreasing every year by approximately 1.75 percent. With an expanding family, the problem is significantly exacerbated.

Within one generation transition, the family's wealth will not support the family at a level that is even close to the prior generations' distributions and overall wealth.

Hence, one understands the classic statement, "rags to riches to rags in three generations"! Although inflation can be a difficult number to measure accurately, ignoring it for longer term financial wealth planning is highly imprudent.

The practice of not measuring the annual costs of inflation in financial planning leads many families to conclude erroneously that if their investment balances are not declining, then the family's wealth is being preserved.

Unfortunately, professional firm investment statements will not show the decline in wealth caused by annual inflation, as they do not account for this measure of real purchasing power loss. Thus, the family receives a flawed view of its *real* wealth—$50 million in wealth today will not have the same purchasing power in later years.

FIST Impact on Multigenerational Wealth Destruction

Year	BOY (2) Investment Balance in Real $'s	# Family Members Supported	EOY (2) Investment Balance Per Family Member in Real $'s	Real $ Spending Per Family Member
1	$50,000,000	1 (Gen 1)	$49,135,939	$1,500,000
2	$49,135,939	1 (Gen 1)	$48,286,810	$1,474,078
3	$48,286,810	1 (Gen 1)	$47,452,355	$1,448,604
4	$47,452,355	1 (Gen 1)	$46,632,320	$1,423,571
5	$46,632,320	3 (Gen 1&2)	$15,275,486	$466,323
6	$45,826,457	3 (Gen 1&2)	$15,011,507	$458,265
7	$45,034,520	3 (Gen 1&2)	$14,752,090	$450,345
8	$44,256,269	3 (Gen 1&2)	$14,497,155	$442,563
9	$43,491,466	3 (Gen 1&2)	$14,246,627	$434,915
10	$42,739,881	6 (Gen 2&3)	$7,000,214	$213,699

(1) Real dollars are the value of dollars after inflation (i.e., true buying power).

(2) BOY = beginning of year; EOY = end of year; balances will be materially different from the actual numbers reported on the investment statement, which are never in real dollars.

The other major element affecting family wealth over time is the growth in family size. Potential family expansion is both hard to predict and awkward to discuss as part of financial planning.

However, family size will affect either the size of the distributions per family member or the amount of wealth that will remain to support future family members, or both. Something must give! If the business maintains the same dollar amount of distributions per family member as family size increases, those distributions will decrease family wealth faster than if distributions per family member were reduced. While this concept is obvious, family leaders seldom consider it—particularly the longer-term implications on multigenerational wealth and sustainability of distributions.

Unfortunately, even with reasonable family spending patterns and good tax management, the impact of inflation and family size make it *impossible* to maintain multigenerational family wealth without cultivating future-generation wealth creators. Factoring in an estimate for estate and gift taxes makes the situation even direr.

Mitigation Strategies

There are six important strategies that can help mitigate the depletion of family wealth for future generations:

1. *Engage* the best of the best estate planning and tax attorneys in order to minimize income and transfer taxes on your wealth. Evaluate use of trusts and prenuptial agreements to protect family wealth transfer upon marital dissolution.

2. *Retain*, do not sell, your family business, unless it is absolutely necessary (most cases are not) or you receive an offer too good to turn down. Require significant growth as a success paradigm, and deploy business capital carefully to be certain it is generating substantial returns.

(Maintaining an existing cash flow business will not sustain family wealth!)

3. *Implement* the ideas outlined in chapter 9 (Avoiding the Family Business Wealth Evaporation Trap).

4. *Allocate* assets and *measure* and *report* investment performance after accounting for management fees, taxes, and inflation; be certain that net investment returns justify paying nondeductible investment management fees *(as of the 2018 Tax Act)*.

5. *Manage* family spending as a *percentage* of assets; prepare annual reports to family members showing wealth *in real dollars* and whether it is accumulating or being consumed.

6. *Encourage* entrepreneurship, self-confidence, personal responsibility, and advanced education (i.e., intellectual capital) with the next generation. Teach older children about business principles, wealth management, and budgeting. When they are young adults, help them understand risk-reward assessment and the difference between playing to "win" versus playing "not to lose."

Developing the Next Generation

A common question from high-net-worth families is, "How do we not mess up our next generation?" This topic triggers intense discussions and understandable parental concerns. Unfortunately, the answer often is, "It depends"—on the particular child and the particular family. Even more challenging, the situation changes over time as children grow up and conditions change.

Understanding children's *feelings* while they're growing up helps parents determine their family's best practices to support and train the next generation. Many parents are surprised to understand the common stresses that children from wealthy families incur growing up are different from those of their children's friends.

The following are examples stated by next-generation family members that may be relevant to your family. These feelings can impact both the next generation's career and sense of self.

- "I can never meet my father's (or mother's) expectations, so why even try!"
- "I can never be as successful as my parents!"
- "I don't want to dedicate my life to the business like my dad; I/we want a balanced work-personal life!"
- "I guess I am supposed to go into the family business or need to go into the family business to get the financial rewards."

These are important issues that children of means experience during childhood and through their twenties. It is best to address them during a child's formative years. These issues, along with discussions on family values and culture, are great topics for family meetings, vacations, or even formal retreats with an outside facilitator.

While family wealth can negatively impact a future generation, there are many examples of high-functioning families with highly productive and successful children. Many of the skills and traits of these successful future generations are initially developed during childhood and early adolescence.

There are several important concepts to consider and implement: collaborative discussions on family values and culture; defining success to include the interests of the child; *experiential learning* about earning money; the importance of saving for future needs;

working and entrepreneurship; gifting to others less fortunate; investing; budgeting; and exposure of children and young adults to people in different economic, social, and ethnic circles.

When developing your plans, remember that *children will learn and retain more from observing parent's behavior than from listening to their words.*

In addition, be certain to include a trustee directive letter in your plans that outline how the children should be treated if something ever happens to the parents.

There are many philosophies of raising children, often within the same extended family! Some wealthy parents, for example, "provide" their next generation with the benefits and privileges they did not receive during their childhood. These parents protect their children and let them know they are "set for life." These children grow up enjoying the best of everything and a certainty of future employment in the family enterprise.

While this method gives children the confidence of financial security, it also can result in a sense of entitlement and arrogance, diminished happiness and fulfillment as adults, and poor self-esteem.

A better approach, refined after years of consulting with owners of many family businesses, balances the privileges their children enjoy while growing up as part of a wealthy family with a range of specific life experiences.

This added exposure to certain life values increases the odds of creating a more self-confident, sensitive, and successful next generation—one that can work effectively and harmoniously with people from a wide range of backgrounds.

The following suggestions provide a starting point for crafting an *individual* strategy for your children.

1. Spend time with your children talking about **family values** and the importance of having meaningful and productive lives—in or outside of your family enterprise. Collectively develop your family's definition of "success" for the next generation.

2. Talk about the **lessons you learned and mistakes you made** while growing up. Share real-life stories of successes and failures of others whom your children may know or know of. Make it "real" so they can learn life lessons vicariously by understanding the experiences of others.

   My grandfather arrived at Ellis Island in 1898. When my father and his eight siblings grew up, they were very poor. As a child, I regularly heard about the old days from all of them. I learned about helping others, working hard, saving money, being honest, the value of an education, and our small family business. I was very lucky—I was able to grow up middle class with the benefit of real-life stories from the economically poor prior generation. That significantly helped mold the person I am today.

   These stories were so valuable that I filmed my father and aunt discussing the old days so that my grandchildren can view them when they are older.

3. During their early adolescence, teach your children skills associated with **earning money**. For example, when they first receive an allowance, tell them the chores that need to be done to earn their allowance (e.g., clear or set the dinner table, make their beds, clean up their bedrooms). This helps build a sense of self-confidence, responsibility, success, and an understanding of the value of money.

4. Later in their childhoods, teach them skills associated with **budgeting and helping others less fortunate**. For example, have your children learn to save money for a future purchase (versus impulse buying), such as a toy or a larger-expense item, like a bicycle. You also can introduce philanthropy by having each child gift some of his or her savings or toys to others less fortunate.

5. During their teen years, have your children get a job where they learn the **value of work**. Certain work activities offer an additional opportunity to learn entrepreneurship, where children must both purchase supplies and deliver services. Examples include lawn mowing, snow shoveling, gardening, car washing, cleaning services, etc.

6. An important life lesson for your children is to **learn from failure**. Many parents "bail out" a child from problems too quickly, which can rob their children of the important experiences gained by overcoming failure and being personally responsible for their actions. Leaning how to rebound from failure and recognizing the lessons learned are important steps in raising responsible children.

7. **Celebrating children's successes** is an excellent way to build their self-confidence and sense of self-worth. Encourage your children to succeed in something of interest to them—whether in academics, the arts, sports, extracurricular activities, or a hobby.

8. During their late adolescence years, introduce more complex issues by opening up a modest investment account, so children can learn about **investing** through their own experiences the value of interest compounding,

risk assessment, and returns on savings. As they gain experience and base knowledge, teach them about investing in different asset classes, the impact of taxes, spending and inflation, and other wealth management concepts.

I remember learning about tax strategies as an eighth grader at the dinner table, albeit a little young but that was my father—all business! In those days, he talked about investment tax credits, double declining depreciation, and creating multiple corporations as corporate income tax rates were reduced for the lower income brackets. Those teaching moments were fifty years ago, yet I still remember them.

9. Depending on the maturity and interests of your children, have them **participate in family meetings**, family business reviews, and meetings with investment advisors. These experiences will be remembered and will help prepare the next generation for leading responsible lives and being good stewards of family wealth.

10. When purchasing items as a parent, teach your children the important lesson that you must **decline or postpone certain purchases** because you do not have the funds in the budget or cannot afford it. When purchasing nice items or experiences, explain how you have been saving up for the expenditure, it is in your budget, and it is something that you value for the family.

11. As a young college student, your child should be on **a budget he or she individually manages** (and sticks to unless a true emergency is encountered, in which case the parents should help the child). Earning spending money (at a

minimum) versus showing up with Mom's American Express card, a new BMW, and an entitlement attitude usually results in better outcomes!

12. Directly expose your child to life **outside the bubble** in which he or she grew up. When children are young and not yet established, they will learn from whomever they encounter, a trait that will continue and be valuable throughout their lives.

In my personal journey, my father "found" me the worst job possible for my college summer employment: laboring in a General Motors foundry (his customer). I joined the United Auto Workers (UAW) union and had to wear an asbestos bib to protect me when taking the top mold off of literally red-hot engine block castings coming down the production line. (The job was so bad, the union negotiated half-hour breaks every hour.)

I learned from being entrenched in the plant about numerous hourly labor jobs and the lives of the people who worked at my side—lessons I vividly remember today.

13. For young adults, **a family bank** is an excellent vehicle to encourage entrepreneurism, risk taking, borrowing money, business planning, and managing a small enterprise—all important skills for future wealth creators or business leaders. The family bank provides a lending or investing vehicle for family members to apply for funding. It should be professionally managed and serve as a training program for future family business leaders.

In conclusion, while perpetuating wealth may be important to your family, there are higher values to consider as well. Teach your children that money, in the end, is important but not the main indicator of success or happiness. Your integrity, work ethic, purpose in life, service to others, and role as loving and supporting spouses, parents, friends, and citizens will bring you much more happiness and personal fulfillment! These items should be important measures for a successful life for any family, but in particular for families of means.

APPENDIX A

Business Planning Checklist

*The following identifies key issues to consider
in developing your business plan.*

1. Executive Overview

» Business overview—major products and services and facilities, future outlook

» Strategic plan overview, including SWOT summary (company strengths, weaknesses, opportunities, and threats)

» Business model (how and where does the company make money)

» Major risks (assessment and mitigation strategies)

» Summary three-to-five-year financial forecast

2. Markets and Opportunities

» Current and future market trends (assessment and problems or opportunities)

» Value proposition of products or services

» Size and growth rates by market segment

» Alternatives to solving market opportunity or problem

» Overview of competition and how competition could react, discussion on company's competitive advantages

3. Marketing, Sales, and Distribution Plan

» Marketing strategy

» Revenue and profitability analyses by customer segment

» Detailed marketing strategies

• Sales strategy and cycle by channel

• Customer-switching costs/barriers

• Initial sales and promotion plan

• Distribution strategy and plan

• Pricing strategy and competitive positioning

• Promotion and advertising strategy

• Market research and validation

» Competitive barriers to entry

» Strategic partnerships and alliances

» Product pricing, features, benefits analysis

» Revenues and margin analysis and unit volume plan (by product, customer, and/or distribution channel)

4. New Products or Services

» Overview of new products/services

» Features and benefits summary (how do new products or services solve a problem or meet an opportunity?)

» Development status of new products or services not ready for launching (remaining steps to full-scale revenue generation)

» Future potential new product, service development plans, opportunities

5. Operations

» Operations strategy (internal operations, outsourcing, joint venture, offshore, etc.)

» Overview of operating plans (facilities, processes, and equipment)

» Capacity analyses (for capacity limiting operations)

» Cost structures and economies of scale

» Critical items sourcing strategy and plan

» Capital requirements plan

» Implementation plan

» Backup or contingency plans

6. Technology and Intellectual Property

» Overview of technology

• Business perspective

• Technological perspective

» Competitive positioning with new technologies

» New technology development plans and milestones, development challenges

» Status of intellectual property protection (licensing, exclusivity, and ownership of IP)

7. Organization and Human Resources

» Future staffing requirements (define skill sets needed for success)

» Recruitment and hiring plans

» Training and development plans

» Organizational changes (responsibility and accountability assignments)

» Management and labor incentive plans

8. Key Milestones

» Short- and long-term business goals and objectives

» Key success factors with measurement targets defined

» Milestones achieved to date

» Future milestones: timeline and measurement criteria

9. Financial Information (information may be prepared by business unit or division or product line and summarized)

» Financial projections including key assumptions and revenue and cost drivers

» Projected revenues (dollars, unit volumes, and margins)

- » Projected operating expenses
- » Projected income statements
- » Projected cash flow statements
- » Project balance sheets
- » Historical and current financial recap

APPENDIX B

Shareholders' Agreement Checklist
For Family Businesses

Introduction

I have identified the following key business issues checklist for families to consider when developing a shareholders' agreement (e.g., operating agreement in limited liability companies, closed corporation agreement in S and C corporations, partnership agreement in partnerships).

An updated shareholders' agreement is particularly important at the beginning of a change in ownership and transition of the business from one generation to the next.

The recommended "output" from these shareholder discussions is a written term sheet to be reviewed and modified by corporate legal counsel. Once a final term sheet is produced, it is strongly recommended that each shareholder has his or her own legal representation review the term sheet prior to drafting documents. The end result is an agreed-upon contractually binding agreement that will define how the owners will function within their family enterprise.

Note: The use of "shareholder" and "shares" should be substituted for "partner" or "member" and "partnership interests" or "member interests" in partnership or limited liability companies.

Governance, Capital, and Key Shareholder Policies

1. Board Representation and Governance

   a. Types of board members: fiduciary or advisory

   b. Size of board

   c. Frequency and location of meetings

   d. Board member term/age limits

   e. Election of board member—How are members elected?

   f. Replacement of board member process

   g. Issues requiring shareholder or supermajority board approval

   h. Compensation of outside directors

   i. Directors and officers (D&O) insurance for directors and officers of company

   j. Board member company indemnification provisions

2. Dividends/Distributions

   a. Policy for personal tax liability distributions (i.e., mandatory quarterly distributions to meet IRS quarterly payment schedules to fund company pass-through tax liabilities)

b. Distributions based upon highest marginal federal, state, and local income tax rates for shareholders

c. Agreement to not negotiate bank or other financial covenants that restrict tax distributions without supermajority (two-thirds) shareholder approval

d. Excess distribution policy (i.e., "distribution of profits"). How determined, approval process, agreement on basic shareholder philosophy—retain to grow business, distribute certain percentage for lifestyle needs, etc.

3. Debt Level Authorization Procedure

a. Requirement for board of director approval.

b. Amount over $_____ requires two-thirds of outstanding shares ratification after board approval?

4. Capital Expenditure and Investment Approvals

a. Requirement for board of director approval

b. Amount over $_____ requires two-thirds of outstanding shares ratification after board approval?

5. Capital Calls and Dilution Guidelines

a. Guidelines for capital calls

b. Preemptive rights for shareholders

c. When additional capital is needed, provisions for capital contributing shareholders if there are also noncontributing shareholders. Possibilities for capital treatment include the following:

- Secured debt with or without conversion rights to equity
- Preferred stock/mezzanine debt
- Equity contribution with dilution of existing ownership
- A stock value pricing formula agreed upon when equity or equity conversion rights are included

6. Sale of Company ("Drag-Along" or "Come-Along/Tag-Along" Rights)

   a. Requirements for board of director approval

   b. Requirements for two-thirds of outstanding shares ratification after board approval

   c. Drag-Along Rights—Nonagreeing shareholders are required to sell their holdings at the same terms and conditions as the agreeing shareholders if a buyer/investor desires to purchase the entire company.

   d. Come-Along/Tag-Along Rights—Any shareholder has the option to force any selling shareholder to include their ownership holdings in any approved partial sale of company stock to a buyer/investor on a pro rata basis so that all owners have a right to sell some or all of their holdings at the same terms and conditions as the initial selling shareholder (and not be stuck with illiquid family business stock with new owners or different ownership percentages)

7. Stock Put Option to Provide Liquidity for Minority Shareholders

    a. At predefined points in time and constrained by a maximum annual and cumulative five-year percentage of shares outstanding, a shareholder could have a "put" option to sell his shares to the company to provide shareholder liquidity; either some, all, or all if the resulting ownership position would be below a minimum threshold level.

    b. The option should be contingent upon terms that protect the viability of the company, including the company's future needs for capital.

    c. Company payment terms need to be defined in an agreement that outlines percentage down payment and maximum annual payments (e.g., as a percentage of free cash flow of the company).

    d. Stock valuation for put option shares, which could be different than normal valuation—include a minority and lack of marketability discount and overall discount to valuation pricing given shares are being put to the company at shareholder's sole option.

    e. Other considerations

        • Time period available for a shareholder to begin process of put shares to company by exercising a "Notice to Put Shares."

        • Other shareholders should have the right to also exercise a "Notice to Put Shares" after receiving written notice that the company received a "Notice to Put Shares" from one or more shareholders.

- If total shares included in the sum of all "Notice to Put Shares" exceed two-thirds outstanding shares, then company will be put up for sale instead of exercising put options.

- If put shares exceed maximum current and cumulative percentage of shares eligible for put, prorate put shares among selling shareholders.

  f. Consider additional discounts to valuation for put shares.

  g. What security, if any, is provided for unpaid obligations for put shares?

  h. Who controls voting rights on put shares until they have been paid for?

Ownership Transfer and Control Issues

  8. Rights of First Refusals

    a. Shareholder desire to sell (receipt of written good-faith offer)

    b. First option to buy: company or other shareholders

    c. Second option to buy: company or other shareholders

    d. Shareholder options to buy typically pro rata

    e. Purchase Price

- Lesser of offer price or price determined under this agreement; or

- Materially equal to offer price

    f. Tag-along rights to other shareholders (see section 6)

g. Need definition of "bona fide" arms-length offer; need to eliminate manipulative bogus offers to buy. Buyer needs to be credible and able to close.

h. Timing of close

i. Payment terms

j. Security for selling shareholders

9. Transfer Restrictions

    a. Restrictions on transfer to non-shareholders without prior written consent of company and shareholders?

    b. Transfer to spouses or children restrictions?

    c. No pledging of stock as security without prior written consent of company and shareholders?

    d. Permitted transfers—to grantor trusts with family members as beneficiaries (if transferee signs shareholders' agreement) and grantor is trustee

    e. Permitted transfers—to family members (if donor signs shareholders' agreement)

    f. Other permitted transfers

10. Triggering Events for Buy-Sell Provisions

    a. Death

- Call option to purchase shares by company or other shareholders?
- Put option for deceased shareholder's estate?
- Terms for call and/or put options (e.g., valuation methodology, discounts, payment terms, security—see sections 11 to 15)

b. Disability

- Define disability in terms of both duration (permanent versus temporary) and activities (total inability to do job?)—consider use of insurance company definition.

- Call option to purchase shares by company or other shareholders?

- Put option for disabled employee?

- Terms for call and/or put options (e.g., valuation methodology, discounts, payment terms, security—see sections 11 to 15)

c. Termination of employment "without good cause" by company

- Call option to purchase shares by company or other shareholders?

- Put option for terminated employee?

- Terms for call and/or put options (e.g., valuation methodology, discounts, payment terms, security—see sections 11 to 15)

d. Termination of employment "for good reason" by employee

- Call option to purchase shares by company or other shareholders?

- Put option for terminated employee?

- Terms for call and/or put options (e.g., valuation methodology, discounts, payment terms, security—see sections 11 to 15)

e. Termination of employment with "good cause" by company

- Call option to purchase shares by company or other shareholders?
- Put option for terminated employee?
- Terms for call and/or put options (e.g., valuation methodology, discounts, payment terms, security—see sections 11 to 15)

f. Voluntary termination of employment including retirement by employee

- Call option to purchase shares by company or other shareholders?
- Put option for terminated employee?
- Terms for call and/or put options (e.g., valuation methodology, discounts, payment terms, security—see sections 11 to 15)

g. Other/involuntary transfers—bankruptcy, divorce, lawsuits

- Call option to purchase shares by company or other shareholders?
- Put option for terminated employee?
- Terms for call and/or put options (e.g., valuation methodology, discounts, payment terms, security—see sections 11 to 15)
- May need mechanism for purchase to occur before court order is final

h. Shareholder deadlock—among shareholders evenly split and unable to negotiate solution

- First resolution attempt using outside board members to mediate

- Mediation
- Formal arbitration—binding or nonbinding
- Sale of business alternatives
    i. Negotiated agreement with pricing, triggers, etc.
    ii. Shareholders sell entire business
    iii. Bring in new investor to buy out one party
    iv. Texas shootout (one party offers a valuation; other party can either buy or sell at that price)
    v. Other

11. Valuation of Shares

    a. "Fair market value" definition for appraisal and guideline for external appraisal firm
    b. Valuation of entire firm as a whole or for specific interests being sold with standard and/or special discounts
    c. Valuation date—recommend as of year ending when triggering event occurred and based upon year-end audited financial statements
    d. Minority, lack of control, lack of marketability discounts—when used, agreed-upon discount percentage, and when not used for following triggers:
        - Death
        - Disability
        - Termination without cause
        - Termination for good reason

- Termination for good cause
- Voluntary termination
- Retirement after certain age (65)
- Other/involuntary transfer (divorce and bankruptcy)
- Shareholder deadlock

e. Use of appraisal firm or formula

12. Requirements/Credentials for an Appraisal Firm

a. Selected firm requires agreement of buying and selling shareholders

b. Industry expertise requirement defined

c. Minimum firm size—regional or national practice

d. Right for selecting additional appraisals upon shareholder disagreement on initial valuation

e. Finalizing accepted valuation when using more than one valuation firm (e.g., selecting two closest appraisals and taking average for final valuation)

f. Who pays for appraisals—first appraisal, additional appraisals

13. Equity Purchase Note Terms and Conditions

a. Down payment defined as dollar or percentage amount, formula, or as agreed upon by outside independent board members?

b. If insurance proceeds are available, down payment could be based upon net insurance proceeds

c. Interest rate (fixed versus floating formula)

d. Term—three, five, seven, or ten years

e. Amortization rate/payment schedule

    i. Frequency of payments

    ii. Equal periodic payments of principal and interest (amortizing loan)

    iii. Interest only, with one or more deferred principal ("bullet") payments

    iv. Equal principal payments, plus accrued interest to date

f. Any covenants on company prior to payoff of shareholder notes?

g. Security for purchase

    i. Pledge of shares—are they voting or nonvoting and by whom?

    ii. Company or shareholder note guarantees; subordination of guarantee

    iii. Any security for guarantee

14. Funding Strategies for Buy-Sell Transaction

a. Use of life insurance as a funding strategy

b. Define whether to exclude or include life insurance proceeds or cash value in determining valuation of selling shares.

c. Protection for company by defining limits on maximum annual payments (i.e., percentage of free cash flow) or debt ratios to limit cash flow used for note payments to buy back shares (i.e., protecting remaining shareholders and company's future)

15. Default and Remedies

    a. Cross-defaults with other agreements

    b. Remedies

    c. Litigation-prevailing party reimburses expenses, including attorney fees

Other Family Business Issues

16. Other Provisions

    a. Noncompetition by seller after closing

        i. Terms

        ii. Prohibited activities

        iii. Geographic scope

        iv. Duration

        v. Setoff for damages

        vi. Confidentiality

    b. If selling shareholder had personally guaranteed corporate debt, how is personal guarantee released; what is remedy/indemnification provision if not?

17. Insurance Provisions

    a. Life insurance purchased on life of each shareholder to fund buy-sell provisions of shareholder agreement?

    b. Disability insurance purchased for family member employees?

    c. Key man life insurance purchased by company to protect shareholder value in case of loss of a key person?

18. Annual Financial Audit or Review Requirements

19. Family Matters

    a. Annual reports and meetings

    b. Visitation rights to board meetings

    c. Access or restrictions to financial information

    d. Establishment, operating guidelines, powers of a family council

APPENDIX C

Family Business Diagnostic Review Checklist

I. Family dynamics assessment

- Overall stakeholder satisfaction and goals alignment
- Understanding of individual needs, desires, and ownership objectives
- Effectiveness of communication and overall transparency; trust and confidence levels among family members; and the general feeling of "connectedness and ability to influence" business

II. Business governance

- Board of directors' effectiveness
- Board member selection criteria and capabilities
- Board meeting operating practices, meeting frequencies, and agenda items

III. Family compensation

- Family employment compensation (base salaries and bonuses)
- Tax distribution practices (for pass-through entities)
- Profit distribution practices
- Balance between compensation versus owner profit distributions

IV. Family governance

- Family policies and constitution
- Family governance organization
- Next-generation guidelines
- Family education programs
- Family networking, communication, and transparency initiatives
- Training and development of next generation

V. Ownership structural assessment

- Shareholder operating or buy-sell agreements
- Family member employment agreements
- Voting rights of ownership versus board versus management

VI. Management structure

- Organizational chart review
- Financial and operating management reporting capabilities

- Business plan review

VII. Succession planning (see chapter 7 for details)

- Financial and "finding purpose" needs of prior generation (if any)
- Existing succession plan review (governance, organization, business plan, risk management, communications)
- Defining roles and rights of family members as owners, board members, managers, and employees

VIII. Family wealth management

- Meeting shareholder financial objectives, desires, and needs as it relates to business financial results, investment returns, investment diversification, liquidity, interest in selling versus retaining business, asset protection, and wealth transfer and estate planning
- Perpetuating multigenerational family wealth

ABOUT THE AUTHOR

George A. Isaac

*Family Business and Family Office Consultant, Board Member
and Advisor, CEO, Executive Coach, and Investor*

GEORGE ISAAC HAS FORTY years of senior executive management, family business, management consulting (prior Deloitte Consulting partner), and private equity investing experience. Isaac is a frequent speaker at national and international business meetings and conferences. He has had numerous articles published on family enterprise issues in international publications, including *CNBC, Inc.*; *Family Business Magazine*; *Directors & Boards* magazine; *Trusts &*

Estate Journal; *Family Office Review*; *Family Office Magazine*; *Wealth Management*; *Business Families Foundation*; *Family Firm Institute*; *Family Office Association*; and *Private Wealth Focus*.

As the former CEO of his third generation family manufacturing, services, and real estate investment businesses, his operating businesses saw six-fold revenue and double-digit earnings growth over eight years before their sale to a NASDAQ-listed public company. In the public company, Isaac served as board and executive committee member, corporate EVP, and divisional CEO before transitioning to consulting full time and overseeing his family's fourth generation real estate business and other investments.

Isaac also is an owner and oversees several Gen 1, 2, and 4 family businesses as well as comanages his Isaac family office, GeoZac Holdings, Ltd. Isaac's investment experience includes participating in the formation of a fund of funds hedge fund, actively investing in private equity and early-stage transactions and investing in public securities and options transactions.

He has served on over twenty-five boards, including fifteen corporate boards. He functioned in lead director roles and participated on executive, audit, compensation, and investment board committees for companies ranging in size from \$30M to \$1BB+. Isaac has consulted on over one hundred client engagements in a variety of industries.

Isaac, credentialed as a Certified Management Consultant (CMC) in 1984, has an MBA with Distinction in Finance and Accounting and a BS in Industrial and Operations Engineering from the University of Michigan. *Additional credentials available at www.GeorgeIsaac.com.*

Management and Leadership Experience

- 25+ years of CEO experience in both manufacturing, service, and real estate–based Gen 2, 3, and 4 family businesses (1988–1997, 1999–present)
- Divisional CEO, corporate senior EVP, executive committee and board member of $1 billion publicly traded company (1997–1999)
- Management consulting partner, Deloitte Consulting; provided general management consulting services in a variety of industries (1977–1988)
- Direct management experience in start-ups, turnarounds, high growth, acquisitions (completed twenty-five acquisitions), and sale of business to both public and private companies
- Numerous active leadership roles in Young Presidents' Organization (YPO) and Chief Executives Organization (CEO) (1989–present)

Board of Director Experience

- Director of two publicly traded companies (manufacturing and financial services)
- Director of thirteen private company boards (several family businesses); meets financial expert requirements for board members
- Chair of audit and compensation committees; member of securities, investment, and executive committees
- Director/trustee of eleven nonprofit boards

Industry Experience

- Manufacturing (chemicals, plastics, metals, capital equipment, recycling, food, and beverage)
- Distribution and logistics (commodity product brokerage, warehousing, logistics, and transportation)
- Financial and professional services (banking, equipment leasing, equipment rentals, investment fund management, consulting)
- Real estate development, investment, and management
- Family business—30+ years of direct hands-on G1–G4 experience as a shareholder, CEO, board member, consultant, executive coach and interim executive

Education and Educational Support

- University of Michigan, BS in Industrial and Operations Engineering (1975)
- University of Michigan, MBA with Distinction 1977)
- Certified Management Consultant (CMC), Institute of Management Consultants (1984)
- Senior Advisor, Subject Matter Expert, and Advisory Board Chair, USC Marshall School of Business Family Business Program (2015–present)
- Member, CNBC—YPO Chief Executive Network (2015–present)
- Member, Advisory Board at University of Michigan's Zell-Lurie Institute of Entrepreneurial Studies at Michigan's Ross School of Business (2001–2006)

- International Board Member, Chief Executives Organization (2012–2016)
- Member, Board of Leaders, University of Southern California's Marshall School of Business (2010–present)

ACKNOWLEDGMENTS

I WANT TO START with recognizing and thanking my wife, Shari Isaac, who recommended I focus my consulting practice on family enterprises. This has allowed me to consult, teach, and write on a subject matter about which I am passionate and care deeply.

I also would like to recognize the many family business clients, including my Isaac family business, that I worked with over the years. It is from working with others that I have learned many of the principles in this book.

I also would like to express my appreciation to the management consulting partners at the Chicago office of Touche Ross (now Deloitte Consulting) for hiring me as a young MBA graduate. After eleven years of training and working on numerous consulting experiences, I was able to leave the partnership well prepared for a rewarding career in business. A special thanks to Anton Petran and Ken Merlau (Ken supported me at Deloitte, Isaac's, and the public company into which the Isaac company merged).

My colleagues Lee Hausner, PhD, Tim Lappen, and Ken Ude, director of the University of Southern California's Family Business Program, have all been very supportive over the years. We have collaborated and presented together at numerous conferences. Ken encouraged me (multiple times) to write this book.

The heavy-lifting thanks goes to Larry Pearson, an internationally recognized and award-winning writer and friend, who spent tireless hours over several months editing this book. His professional skills combined with his significant business experience proved extremely valuable. Larry's continuous encouragement to "go for it" resulted in a much more significant outcome than was originally intended.

And my final and heartfelt thanks go to Jamie Cornell, a Young Presidents' Organization (YPO) colleague, who volunteered to peer review this book. Jamie, a seventh-generation family enterprise executive, is a life-long student, mentor, advisor, teacher, and expert in the field. He provided great insight and contributions to the final document.